Jonathan Winters . . . After The Beep

Jonathan
Winters...

After The Beep

collected by **Jim B. Smith**

A PERIGEE BOOK

Perigee Books
are published by
The Putnam Publishing Group
200 Madison Avenue
New York, NY 10016

Library of Congress Cataloging-in-Publication Data

Winters, Jonathan.
    Jonathan Winters . . . After the beep/collected by Jim
B. Smith.
        p. cm.
    I. Smith, Jim B. II. Title. III. Title: Jonathan Winters
. . . After the beep.
PS3573.I545J6   1989   88-34146 CIP
818'.5402—dc19
ISBN 0-399-51535-6

Book design by Sheree L. Goodman

Printed in the United States of America

1 2 3 4 5 6 7 8 9 10

Acknowledgments . . .

Thanks
Jonathan, Eileen, Jay and Lucinda
For the good times

Jessica Kaye
For your encouragement

Darin Maurer
For your great enthusiasm and honesty

Pam, Beverly, Gene
For your support

Tina Isaac
For your sunshine

Sean Kelly
For your expert help and direction

Trish Todd
For opening the magic door

Lindley Boegehold
For letting me share
the *real* Jonathan Winters

Contents ...

King of the Hill ...

Jonathan Winters might be the funniest person in the world. I think he is. And everyone seems to agree that he's a genius. ("If I'm a genius, Mr. Smith," says Jon, "why am I not working more often?")

He's a movie actor, a best-selling author, a stand-up comic, and acclaimed painter . . . and on his many, many television appearances, he's made millions of us laugh till it hurts with his outrageously real—and surreal—characters and insights.

Yet everyone who knows Jon personally, or has worked with him, will tell you that there's a part of him, an aspect of his extraordinary talent, that the public has never seen . . .

Mr. Winters and Mr. Smith on the beach in Malibu, California. 1956.

Introduction . . .

Jonathan Winters and I met in Hollywood during rehearsal for a 1954 NBC television special. I was working the show as an actor, and Jonathan was doing a stand-up comedy routine, "The Hunter as Seen Through the Eyes of His Dog." Jon portrayed both the trigger-happy hunter (with sound effects) and the more sensible retriever who wound up covering his eyes with his paws. Everyone on the set agreed his performance would steal the show.

An actor-singer friend of mine, Buck Young, was working the special and he coaxed me into putting J.W. on a little. Buck suggested that I do my Walter Brennan impression for Jon, but as I approached the magic man I instinctively fell into one of my back-home rural characters.

"Mr. Winters, my name is Jim Smith, and me and the missus come on out here on a tour bus and I . . . ."

Winters raised an eyebrow and threw me a haughty star-type look. "Where you from, Mr. Smith?"

"Dow City, Iowa," I said. "The tour guide was just leadin' us down the hall out there, and I looked in and seen you. I've seen you on TV and everything, and I just told the missus that I was goin' to run into the studio here, and go right on up to ya! I broke away before anyone could stop me and, well, here I am!"

Jon was really enjoying the character . . . I had punched his most accessible and responsive button!

"Well, what do you want, Mr. Smith? An 8 × 10 glossy that glows in the dark?"

I scuffed my shoes a little. "No sir, Mr. Winters, just to stand in your presence is the biggest thrill I ever had!"

Jon exploded with laughter. "Where did you ever get that

character? I do one like that. I got mine from some guys around Dayton!"

I told him that these same guys are in Dow City every Wednesday and Saturday night, and that I'd grown up with them. Jon pushed to find out more about my home town. I explained that it had a population of about 565 folks forty years ago, and the tally was the same today, including some jackrabbits. Jonathan loved it. We found a common ground in that good ol' boy character, and the beginning of a friendship that has endured for thirty-five years.

Jon went into a little bit about Dayton and his last trip back home. He'd gone to see his buddy Ben, who owned a bait shop. Jon has always loved to fish, but he was also fascinated with the bait shop clientele. Ben greeted Jon and remarked that he hadn't seen him around for quite a while. "Well, I got pretty lucky, Ben, I've been out in California working on television," Jon responded. Ben's eyes lit up. "Hey, Jon, maybe you could take a look at my old Zenith . . . the picture just don't look right no more!"

Jonathan had come to California only to work on a summer replacement show, and he was preparing to round-trip it back to New York when the network cut him off at the pass with a *Colgate Comedy Hour* contract. I was delighted with this development, since I worked that show almost every week, and I knew that Jon's presence would mean more fun and games.

The *Comedy Hour* was rehearsed and telecast at the magnificent old El Capitan located just north of Hollywood and Vine. The El Cap was once the home of the famous "Ken Murray Blackouts" and many other successful stage presentations. It wasn't your average TV studio, but a real theater with a large seating capacity. The stage area was made to order for Jon's between-takes improvisations in front of a live audience. Much to the dismay of the writers, his impromptu routines were usually funnier than the scripts. Jon's off-the-top-of-his-head bits soon became the talk of the industry.

Jon's and my friendship blossomed during our extracurricular activities. Together we sniffed out all the local hangouts, and we soon became familiar faces in most of the famous—and infamous—Hollywood nighteries. Our MO was to get a running start in Hollywood after a show or rehearsal and stop at every oasis until we reached a place called The Cottage, in Malibu. Then we would make a U-turn and rediscover all of the same bars in reverse order.

Jon gave incredible improvised one-man shows at every stop. I don't recall that we were ever asked to pay for a drink. Curiously, Jon was consuming a tremendous amount of alcohol, but I never saw any evidence that the booze was affecting him in any way. I can truthfully say that I never saw Jon drunk. The stuff seemed to make him faster, sharper, and kept him going . . .

One morning, I picked Jon up at the Beverly Hills Hotel, where he was staying, and drove straight to a Sunset bar called Googies. We had spent a long hard night on the Strip and felt we needed an eye-opener. We found Googies' doors locked, but the manager recognized Jon and let us in. He explained that it was only 9:30 A.M., and that they couldn't legally serve liquor until 10:00. We nursed coffees until the magic hour—then Jon moved back of the bar and began the greatest show on earth. Word of this spontaneous comedy combustion spread, and the saloon soon filled with enthusiastic spectators. We were there for hours, and I think that if I hadn't tempted Jon with promises of more big fun down the line, we'd have spent all our time frolicking at Googies.

Our next stop wasn't far away. Soon after we were inside, Jon spotted Barry Sullivan behind a pair of shades, and I should have guessed what was coming. Grinning happily, Jon introduced himself to Sullivan, who reacted stiffly. Jon interpreted this reaction as "star stuff," which confirmed the impression given by the dark glasses.

"You know, Barry, some of us try all of our lives to be recognized, but here you are hiding. It's confusing to me. You know, the dark shades don't make it. What you should do is get a hood with just a couple of slits for your eyes, and nobody'd recognize you." Sullivan clenched his teeth and I reached for Jon's elbow again. "It's time for us to depart, Mr. Winters," and out we went. Jon never picks on anyone unless he deserves it. I guess he thought Barry Sullivan deserved it . . .

Jon is always appreciated by other performers. In those days, our favorite eating establishment was the Bit of Sweden, a superstar hangout. What we liked about the place was that it featured complimentary buckets of meatballs at the bar. What could be better than good, fast, free food—that didn't interfere with our drinking? We would usually empty two or three buckets and split. But it wasn't a bad deal for the Bit either, because Jon would always perform at the bar, so business boomed. One night Randolph Scott was seated at the bar and Bing Crosby was tucked away in a booth nearby. Jon approached Scott in the tentative way of a blind man. Scott played along, as Jon explored his entire anatomy with his "seeing hands." At the appropriate moment, Jon exploded, "It's Randolph Scott! Oh my God, I've touched a superstar!" At this apparent confirmation of his legendary virility, Scott fell apart with mirth, and Crosby laughed so hard, he shook the booth.

Most comedians like to play the big room in a hotel, but Jon has done some of his best work in hotel lobbies—such as the Polo Lounge in Beverly Hills. One evening, he encountered an internationally known oil magnate there. This fellow, whom I shall not name (for obvious reasons), was married to a one-time goddess of the silver screen—a glamorous European import who in her younger days had done some pretty explicit nude-in-the-water scenes. This was a Hollywood secret, which means everybody in the business knew all about it.

The Oil King started heckling Jon, to no effect. Then he got cantankerous. Show business, he said loudly, was a joke. *He* was a self-made man, and was worth millions. Jon asked if he had it on him. "Anybody can talk about the green stuff, but if you want to impress folks, you should carry it around with you." Mr. Petro-bucks blew a gasket. "Do you know who I *am*? I'm married to H***** ******!" Jon nodded. "Oh, yeah. She's the swimmer, right?" The oil man was held down just long enough for us to make another timely exit . . .

One afternoon, we fell by Nicodel's Bar in Hollywood. We'd

just finished rehearsal for a *Comedy Hour* that was to be aired live the following night. Jon, who is an ex–Marine, spotted an active-duty leatherneck sitting at the bar and decided to have some fun. He instantly assumed the role of Paul Precious, a very prissy pacifist. "Paul" introduced himself to the Marine and began holding forth on the horrors of war. The Marine was buying it all the way. Then Jon went too far—with Paul's outrageous account of how he had evaded the draft . . . The enraged serviceman threw a haymaker. Down went Jon, and by the time he recovered, several of us had jumped in between the adversaries. Jon (who weighed in at 240 and who could—I knew—handle himself) gave the Marine a baleful stare and, still in his Paul Precious voice, hissed, "Now *that* was in *very* bad taste!"

Of course, we all broke up, and just about that time, the Marine recognized Jon. The poor guy almost cried—and spent the rest of the day buying drinks and apologizing, until he and Jon wound up arm in arm singing the Marine Hymn.

Next day Jon arrived for the *Comedy Hour* shoot sporting a big, beautiful black eye. The producer, Ernie Glucksman, was real upset. But Shotgun, the veteran makeup man, took charge. He prescribed a piece of raw beefsteak for Jon to hold over his eye, after which he would perform his makeup magic. The fact that Jon's wife, Eileen, didn't call in distress after the show was living proof that the shiner didn't read on camera!

Eileen was back home, in Mamaroneck, New York. Jon's schedule was set for him to work a couple of *Comedy Hour* shows on the West Coast and then fly back home. I used to chauffeur him from the hotel to the airport in my 1946 Chevy.

The trip from Beverly Hills to LAX usually took us about three days. There were so many watering holes to check out en route, and of course Jon had to do his routines in each establishment. He would keep asking me how much time we had to make the flight until I told him we had missed it. Then he seemed to relax, and always suggested that we go back to the hotel and reschedule at the Polo Lounge! Eileen would call eventually and ask why her husband hadn't made the flight, and Jon's typical reply, in a weak raspy voice, was that he had the flu and was lying there in a pool of sweat. She would ask if he had seen the doctor, and J.W. would explain that his buddy Jim was taking good care of him. Eileen would be all sympathy and concern. It was a great act—while it lasted.

We arrived at the Beverly Hills Hotel one morning around seven, after an all-nighter. We were beat. As we got to Jon's room, the phone rang. It was Eileen, calling from the Los Angeles airport and furious that Jon wasn't there to meet her. Now, Jon had entirely forgotten that Eileen was coming—but he explained that the show had scheduled an early morning meeting and he'd had no way of notifying her. He was apologetic. He was reasonable. He suggested she grab a cab. And we both had thirty minutes to shower, shave, and look like we were wide awake and fresh as daisies. It was a real acting challenge for two hung-over players.

But it was good to meet Eileen. She was (and is) most attractive and genuine—an honest-to-goodness down-to-earth person. And we didn't fool her for one second, as she played her part—very understanding and upbeat. Jon and I now had a case of the guilties to go with our hangovers, but we all went out for a big breakfast in Hollywood. Very charming, very chatty, and alert. Then I went home to crash for twelve hours.

Jonathan was fast becoming a whirlwind of success. Hollywood honored him by placing his "star" and name on the Vine Street Walk of Fame. I was much more excited than Jon. I bubbled to him that he had made it . . . his name was there among the greatest show-business celebrities in history. Jon put it all into a typical Winters perspective: "There will be millions walking on the star, Mr. Smith. Well, that's okay . . . people have been stepping on me all of my life. Why should they stop now?"

Jon had experienced a meteoric rise to fame in a very short period of time. All of the attention and success didn't swell his ego one bit. He has never succumbed to the Hollywood vanity scene. Paradoxically, I believe that Jon's humility actually contributed to his early emotional problems. His modest self-image had a tough time keeping pace with his press releases, and this dilemma exerted a terrific pressure on the man. The bars, booze, and party scenes offered Jon a respite from that pressure, and—as it turned out—the price for the temporary reprieve was too high.

Anyone lucky enough to spend an evening with Jon in those days was almost as impressed by his ability to hold his liquor as by his brilliant improvised comedy routines. But I, who spent *many* evenings with him, was worried about what drink was doing to him. His established morning routine was to brush his loosening teeth . . . and then throw up.

Jonathan returned to New York for more television appearances (Jack Paar, Steve Allen, Garry Moore), leaving me behind for some long overdue rest and recuperation.

Back East, his drinking increased proportionately with his success, and the word was out that Jon was headed for serious trouble. He has since told me that a couple of alcohol-related events convinced him he had to change course. In the first, he drove into town to pick up a loaf of bread and woke up the next morning in a Chicago hotel room, with no idea how he'd got there. He says he knew then that booze was taking over his life.

Some weeks later, there was a party at the Winterses' suburban home. It was obvious to everyone that Jon was not himself that night. He was less than hospitable with his guests, and at one point abruptly retreated to his backyard to get away from everyone. According to Jonathan, he was lying down on the grass, looking at the stars, when something happened that changed his life.

Jon, who is very private about some things, will only characterize that event as "a religious experience." He got up, walked back into the house, and told Eileen that he was never going to drink again. And he hasn't touched a drop of alcohol since that night in 1959.

Jon's drinking stopped but, unfortunately, trouble of another kind was waiting for him just around the bend. He was booked into the famous Hungry i nightclub in San Francisco. Jon did three shows a night—and in addition met with needy Alcoholics Anonymous members at all hours. He was substituting coffee for booze now, and setting new world records for caffeine consumption. Late one night he went right into orbit.

After his third show, Jon—an insomniac—headed for Fisherman's Wharf to relax. An old ship was anchored there, and Jon decided he was its captain. Within minutes J.W., salty old sea dog, began issuing suitably nautical orders to his "crew"—in this case, a caretaker on the dock. Lacking an appreciation for the art of free-form improvisation, the guy got scared and called the cops. The police arrived, recognized Jon, and were willing to laugh it off—but now Winters began to insist that he was "John Q" from outer space. And I mean *insist*. The laughing stopped, and Jon was taken down to the station for a misdemeanor booking. The precinct desk captain asked Jon to state his name for the record. "John Q from outer space!" he proclaimed.

Supervised rest worked wonders on him. Jon was soon released from custody and flew home to Mamaroneck. The newspapers go a hold of the story, however, and made quite a spectacular event of it, claiming that Jon had climbed the mast of the ship and refused to come down. To this day, Jon takes great exception to those journalistic exaggerations. "Can you see me climbing a mast, with this round body?"

Jon soon returned to California for a booking at the then popular and prestigious Mocambo, on the Sunset Strip in LA. His hotel was within walking distance of the club, and we met in his room for dinner before his first show. The new booze-free Winters was, if anything, quicker and funnier than before. So much for my theories about alcohol giving him more wit and energy. But something was obviously wrong.

He was terribly intense, restless, hyper. The humor was always there, of course, but J.W. was jumping from subject to subject in rapid succession—always a bad sign for Jon. The club bookings, I realized now, were posing a threat to the emotional well-being of my friend.

He snatched up a piece of parsley from his plate and announced that it was a little tree from Dow City, Iowa. He presented me with this "award from my home town" while delivering a fitting and remarkably funny speech. I laughed, and then reminded Jon that we were running late. Motivated more by his fetish for promptness than anything else, he threw on his blue blazer and we were off. As we made our way down the hotel corridor, Jon spotted an emergency fire hose. He grabbed it and started barking orders into the nozzle: "Now hear this, now hear this!" I believe that this was the "captain" of the ship in San Francisco Bay that night.

We were walking down Sunset toward the Mocambo when Jon suddenly bolted into the middle of the street. Horns squealed and howled. J.W. was standing stock-still in front of a Bentley. Dodging traffic, I ran over to Jon. The driver of the Bentley, who seemed to recognize him, was laughing and pleading with Jon to let him go. Traffic was roaring by on either side of us. As calmly as I could, I urged J.W. to come off the street . . . but Jon was pointing at the "B" emblem on the front of the Bentley radiator. "What does that say?" he demanded.

Sensing imminent disaster, I blurted, "It stands for Bentley." "No, no!" Jon assured me, "it stands for St. Bernadette!"

I was about to admit that I wasn't too up on my saints when something quite amazing happened. A small but husky young man dashed into the street and literally tackled Jon. Then in one motion, he lifted my substantial friend up and carried him back to the curb. He set him down, smiled, and said, "You'll be all right, Jonathan," and disappeared into the crowd that had gathered.

I never saw him again—but I sometimes wonder if St. Bernadette ever sends guardian angels . . .

Jon and I continued our rather unusual walk to the Mocambo. Along the way he was laughing about the street incident as if it were a comedy routine.

His manager, Marty Goodman, joined us in the dressing room before the first show. Jon was rambling and still very hyper. Out of nowhere, he became obsessed with unidentified flying objects. Marty shot a "What do we do?" look at me, and I shrugged. On stage, Jon continued his meditations about UFOs and their possible occupants, "people with glass heads." The audience didn't know what to make of it, and became restless. Jon, sensing their uneasiness, went quickly into his famous baseball pitcher routine and soon had them roaring with laughter.

As marginal as he was, Jon was still razor-sharp. A middle-aged fellow and a young lady-of-the-night type entered the club noisily while the show was on. Jonathan read the situation instantaneously. For some reason, the couple were given seats close to the stage. The young woman was well in her cups and began heckling Winters: "You're too fat to be funny . . . the prices in here are funnier than the act!" Jon signaled the lighting man to put a spot on the couple's table, then leaned down and spoke directly to the girl: "Please, ma'am. I've only got thirty-five minutes up here to make my living. *You've* got the rest of the night." The audience howled and Jon finished the set, uninterrupted.

After the first show, we gathered again in the dressing room, where Jon wasn't making much sense. Abruptly he turned and charged out the exit, into the night. Marty and I looked at each other stunned, then ran after him. Outside we saw Jon scramble up a mound of dirt at a construction site. Standing on top, he declared loudly that he was "King of the Hill!" I started up, hoping to coax him down, but Jon yelled in a frightened way, "No, no! Don't come any closer! I'm telling you, I'm *King of the Hill!*" I forced a laugh and said, "If the King doesn't come down off his throne and do the next show for his court, the King is not going to get paid." Jon laughed, and step-danced back down.

He got through the late show by the grace of God, but it was obvious to all of us that he needed medical attention. Eileen was notified, and when she flew out from New York next morning, I was there to give her an update. She called a doctor, Jon was given medication to help him sleep, and I departed.

I was surprised to receive a phone call from Jon the next day. He had logged fifteen hours of solid sleep, and now sounded completely normal. The last few days had seemed like a dream, he said. He just needed some down-time and he'd be good as new. He was heading back East, going home. "Let's keep in touch, Mr. Smith," he said.

And stay in touch we did—by phone—until 1960, when

Jonathan convinced me that I should head East and test my acting talents in New York. He and Eileen invited me to stay with them and their two children, Jay and Lucinda, until I found my own place.

In their home, I discovered the *real* Jonathan Winters for the very first time. Without alcohol or on-the-road pressures to cloud reality, I saw a Winters who is an ultra-sensitive man . . . with a lot of little boy in him. There was abundant evidence that Jon had come from a broken home. I could see the scars—a man who overreacts to the slightest hurt, a child within shouting, "Look at me! Pay attention to me! Love me!" Sure signs of a painful childhood.

Jon used to find solace in the attic of his suburban home, where he would retire to ponder, to write and paint. The room was adorned with papier-mâché birds suspended from the ceiling. J.W. has always loved birds, and they feature in many of his paintings. If you look real close, you will usually find one upside down, or one with a key in its side. Typical Winterism . . .

One day, when Jon and I were in his loft, I asked him if he would paint a picture for me sometime. An hour later, he presented me with a beautiful painting of a Polynesian girl holding a brilliant bouquet of flowers in her hands. The painting was inscribed, "To Jimmie. When she drops her flowers, you'll see the damndest pair of pearl handles you've ever seen! Jonathan, 1960."

New York is a rough city for an actor, and the Winters home was a perfect place for me to relax and lick my wounds after days of "cattle call" auditions. Jon and Eileen were wonderful, and their kids made my adopted family beautifully complete.

There were many social gatherings in the couple's Mamaroneck home. Abstinence made Jonathan's heart grow fonder, and at those parties he had more fun than anyone! Durward Kirby, Art Carney, and their wives were frequent guests. Pals were constantly arranging friendly "shoot-outs" between Jon and the top comedians of the day. Suffice it to say that the King of the Hill was never dethroned in those comic confrontations.

I remember a day when Jon answered the phone, spoke briefly, then returned to the den. I casually asked who had called. It was Jackie Gleason, said Jon, pitching a new television series idea. Jackie was proposing a show in which he would star along with Buddy Hackett and Jonathan. Jon had asked, "What are you going to call it, 'The Three Little Pigs'?" He flashed that impish grin. "Gleason hung up on me!"

Jon has always loved to fish, and he and I used to rent a small boat to assault the local bay areas. You get to know a guy pretty well when you throw a line in the water with him. I came to believe that Jon was, and would forever be, a prisoner of his own unique talent. A part of Jon wants to hang out with friends and whittle; the other part demands that he perform, and exercise those talents. I think that my friend J.W. has always suffered from that conflict.

And when it comes to performing, Jon prefers "street scenes," doing on-the-spot improvisations—in the local drugstore, in a hotel lobby, on an airplane—rather than on stage or on camera. But the pay is better under the lights.

Early in 1963 (I had moved to my own place in town by then—not even the hospitable Winters family could entertain a *permanent* house guest) Jon signed for the film *It's a Mad, Mad, Mad, Mad World*. The character of the truck driver was a variation on the "good ol' boy" he often adopts in his street scenes, and it remains his all-time favorite movie role. Hollywood now "discovered" Jonathan Winters, and he and the family moved to California so he could star in the bizarre black comedy *The Loved One* in '64 and the delightful *The Russians Are Coming! The Russians Are Coming!* the following year.

But movies—which involve a highly organized, tightly structured process—are hardly the ideal medium for J.W. For one thing, he hates to memorize lines, and says he can't. Jonathan is a creator, not an interpreter. He is at his best improvising a scene, but in films that freewheeling technique creates problems for the editors as well as the other actors. Learning lines, then standing by for setups and retakes is not the Winters style. As he says, "How many times can you ask

a sprinter to run a hundred-yard dash and keep winning the
race?!"

One Winters film of which I, at least, have fond memories
is *Viva Max!* a 1968 comedy about the recapture of the Alamo, in which Jon's costars were Peter Ustinov, Harry Morgan, and—by happy coincidence—yours truly.

We began shooting on location, in San Antonio, Texas.
In off-hours, Jon and I found some amazing ways to spend
our per diem money. One afternoon we stopped at a bar-
restaurant famous for Rocky Mountain Oysters—you know,
those little round things that are found on the underside of
male cattle. I don't know about Jon, but it was my first and
last experience with those delicacies. They taste all right, but
the images one conjures up while eating them leave much to
be desired. And their consistency . . . let's just say that if one
of them accidentally rolled off the table, I'd look for it to
bounce!

Jon and I had both consumed vast quantities of iced tea
on that hot day, and our relief calls came at about the same
time. As we entered the men's room, my practiced eye told
me that it was a basic three-urinal setup. A large Texan had
already assumed "post position" number two. Jon took the
outside position on the left and I took the right. The cowboy
was listing slightly to starboard, and otherwise indicating by
his behavior that he had overdone it with spirited beverages.
I had no sooner started to fulfill my purpose in being there
when the Texan looked over at me with the funniest and most
reverent look I'd ever seen and whispered, "That's Jonathan
Winters next to me!" I smiled and nodded. "I never dreamed
that I would *ever* be takin' a leak with Jonathan Winters!" said
he. And I replied, "You have *arrived,* my friend!"

Silent laughter shook Jonathan until his aim was effected.
As Jon and I retreated from the room, the cowboy still had
that awestruck grin on his face—as if he intended to savor
his experience forever. We collapsed with laughter the moment we left.

The making of *Viva Max!* went smoothly—until we got to
the Alamo itself. The Daughters of the American Revolution
resented the film crew making comic use of the hallowed

grounds, and began to put pressure on us. They egged vehicles, and had subpoenas served almost every day. The producer ran out of patience . . . he pulled the plug and removed the entire enterprise to—of all places—Rome, Italy.

Jon's humor recognizes no borders and knows no boundaries. The Italians loved him. He could not, of course, speak their language, but he mastered the Roman accent instantly. The locals thought that Jonathan was speaking Italian until they listened closely—then they would howl with glee at his perfect imitation.

Jonathan and Peter Ustinov made quite an off-the-set comedy team; I think their IQs must be in about the same astronomical range. Jon was more the pure improviser, while Peter was more the storyteller, and their combined talents provided many hilarious moments for the cast and crew until the picture was wrapped.

As with most Winters movies, the best laughs were left offscreen. I still can't help believing that somewhere out there is a film property perfectly suited to Jonathan's unique performing skills . . . And brilliant as his on-stage performances always are, neither are nightclubs the ideal venues for Jon. His last major club appearance was in 1972, as the big-room headliner at the Hilton International in Las Vegas. Jon would be following Elvis Presley's stint there.

Even so, the Hilton rolled out the red carpet for us small fry (at Jon's invitation, I was acting as his road manager on this gig). We were limo'd to our palatial quarters and told to order anything we desired, which we didn't hesitate to do. Imagine a pair of grown men (in Jon's case, *fully* grown) attempting that very afternoon to OD on room-service Beluga caviar . . .

That night, we attended Presley's final show, and Elvis interrupted his act to give Jon about fifteen minutes' worth of accolades. *Mad, Mad World,* he said, was his favorite film, and the scene in which Jon wrecks a filling station was the funniest thing he had ever seen.

Jon and I were invited back to Elvis's dressing room afterward. Elvis entered wearing an Oriental mask—a funny and unexpected bit in Jon's honor, and the King of Rock and the King of the Hill hit it off beautifully.

After an hour or so, as Jon and I were saying our good-byes, Elvis observed that people thought he was a prisoner. "That's really crazy," he said. "Hey, man, last Sunday I spent two hours on my dirt bike!"

As we walked, in silent reflection, down the long con-course that led to the stage exit, Jon turned to me. "You know, Snuffy, the guy really is a prisoner. He thinks that two hours on a dirt bike is total freedom . . . it's sad!" I nodded in agreement—and couldn't help but think that Jon too was feeling trapped by his own talents, by his need to perform. He would rather have been anyplace than headlining in Vegas.

Jon's act was a smash, the top draw on the Strip. And he was making over $100,000 a week. But the two-show-per-night commitment was a strain, and the idea that he was on the leash for two weeks was in itself a pressure.

Every night he would assure me that he was only going to do a thirty-minute set, and asked me to give him a flash-light signal at the half-hour mark. Each night he ignored my cue, and went for another forty-five minutes. He can't turn that talent off when it's flowing . . .

At the end of the engagement, Jon decided that he was done with nightclub appearances forever. "It's just not worth the price . . . any price!"

And then, of course, there was television. For over four decades Jon has made literally thousands of TV appear-ances—in his own series, as the star of dozens of specials, and as a guest on many more—but, like film, the medium restricts him. Scripts limit his creativity, cues inhibit his spon-taneity.

As far as talk shows go, Jon was never fond of the format, and he has even less enthusiasm for it these days. He will occasionally submit to appearing on the Johnny Carson show—because he likes Johnny and because the show is taped only about two miles from his home. But there is more to it than convenience: Before the show, Carson always comes back to Jon's dressing room and spends time with him. That courtesy is greatly appreciated by Jon. (You'd be surprised at the number of talk show hosts who do not extend that consideration to their guests—they're the ones Jonathan Winters has never appeared with again).

A couple of years ago, Jon began writing short stories, and one day, when we were discussing ways to market them, I suggested he pitch the idea on some talk shows.

"Talk shows are bad news, Mr. Smith," he growled. "The host gets twenty million bucks and the guest gets four hundred. I haven't done a talk show for five years and I don't intend to do another one!"

"What about the exposure?" I asked.

"I don't need exposure, Mr. Smith."

"What about your short stories, Mr. Winters?"

That did it.

Jon appeared on a Letterman show, then followed up with Carson. Random House signed him up fast for *Winters' Tales*, which quickly became a best-seller.

Author, actor, comedian, painter—Jon's unique talents have been displayed in so many ways . . . But those of us lucky enough to know Jon personally have always felt that there's another side, another angle, another depth to his comic genius that's never been captured. He's at his very best in private, away from lights and cameras and paying audiences, free of scripts, cues, commercial breaks, sets, stages, and studios. Then the "spontaneous and unrehearsed" genius really comes forward.

Eileen Winters, myself—everyone close to him—has always agreed that this special part of Jon could be recorded only by some uncensored, private, and utterly uninhibiting means, a concept that seemed impossible—until the telephone answering machine came along.

I was one of the first people in the country to buy one of the contraptions, and I did so strictly with Jonathan Winters in mind. Sure enough, J.W. began to leave wild and wonderful character messages on the machine as soon as I set it up. Over the years, I have collected more than three thousand of these unprompted, unpredictable free-form flights of the Winters imagination.

When I informed Jon that I was saving his messages, he thought I was "shuckin' [him] a little." Not until he read the transcribed material was he convinced that I was, indeed, collecting them. It was curious to observe Jon's complete detachment as he read the transcriptions of his own extemporaneous creations. Predictably, he didn't remember many of the bits, and would smile or laugh as if discovering the work of some brilliant stranger.

I suggested to J.W. that he could sprinkle a little sunshine around this old troubled world if this material were published. Jon stroked his chin while he turned the idea around in his mind. "Well, the messages aren't *sacred,* Mr. Smith . . ."

So here are some of my friend Jon's improvisations— some of the characters, stories, scenes, and observations that have visited his amazing mind. I believe they comprise the elusive missing piece of Jonathan Winters' legacy.

Jim B. Smith
Playa Del Rey, California
September 1988

Jim Smith and Jonathan Winters in Pensacola, Florida. 1986.

Grandma Frickert . . .

Grandma "Maudie" Frickert is Jonathan's most fa-mous character. She is an irreverent old gal who is still somewhat occupied with sexual fantasies. This character was inspired by Jon's Aunt Lou. Jon loved her dearly, and his daughter, Lucinda, carries her name. Jonathan keeps saying that he is going to retire Grandma Frickert one of these days. "I don't want to be buried in the dress, Mr. Smith," he tells me. In spite of Jon's concern for Grandma's retirement, she still speaks out occasionally.

BEEP This is Grandma Frickert and . . . ahhh . . . I wanted to call ya. I received your card . . . God Love ya. Ahh, for you to remember my eighty-seventh birthday . . . oh my God, how sweet . . . I thought I'd have a stroke . . . nobody's written to me. 'Course, everybody's dead all around down here at . . . at . . . Merleyville . . . They're all gone. I don't know if you recall . . . I married a young boy this last fall, right after we had that bad blight? And all our trees are dead. Oh, it was a tremendous loss, and I went into a deep depression. I've been a manic-depressive since I was in my late forties. I think that's what caused me to marry seven or eight times. But, I married a young boy from Plainville. About a good five miles from here is where he growed up, and he's twenty years old, and he's hard as *cee*-ment! God, I mean he's got a body on him . . . I'd like to put him out front and put a hook in his hand and pull that Belgian mare up to him . . . he's just . . . he's a wonderful boy. He can pitch hay higher and further than any hired hand the mister ever had. And he's been so good to me. Ya know, my back was broken . . . ahh . . . he gunned the jeep here . . . it was two Sundays ago, and we were on our way to church, and he gunned it . . . I told him not to . . . these Ford Broncos are good jeeps, but he gunned it, and throwed me out of the back, and my back is broken in five places. I held up a picture to him. Well, I taught him a lesson . . . I showed him a picture of Pat Summerall, the man who sells them True Value things. You know, the football player. Pat had a hammer in his hand, and I had a hammer in my hand, and when the boy, Emry . . . the boys' name is Emry . . . and when Emry looked at the ad, I hit him with that hammer. He's not right, but he's still good to me and that's all I need is for somebody to come upstairs at night, you know, and at least lay close to me . . . and uhh . . . I kind of, you know, have to get his attention . . . like in the old joke . . . I hit him with that hammer, and he'll do most anything, God love him. But thanks so much again for the birthday card . . . that was sweet of ya. I was hopin' for a call but the card was cute. I don't know . . . it rained that week, bad, and of course it rained right into the envelope, and into the lettering. So I couldn't make out what ya said, but I seen your name there below. Thanks so much. God love ya, and Emry says hello. I'd put him on, but ya know when you been hit by a hammer almost every night for the last 37 days . . . there ain't nothin' much for ya to say!

Chester Honeyhugger Arrives . . .

Chester Honeyhugger is a sweet, lovable, precocious little boy we can all relate to. Jonathan's childhood was lacking in parental love and affection and part of him is still trying to relive the things he missed while he was growing up. Maybe, through Chester, he enjoys a "second time around."

BEEP Hi, this is Chester . . . Chester Honeyhugger! Do you remember me? I'm Aunt Louise's son? And, umm, I'm seven and a half years old . . . Well, I'm gonna be eight in April. You're probably wondering right now where I am. I'm in Torrance. I don't know how close that is to where you are. I know you're in Los Angk . . . Los Angeles. But my plane landed at John Wayne Airport. Incidentally, I didn't see John Wayne. Anyway, I have my doggy, and a change of clothes . . . my Doctor Dentons, which are a full pajama suit with feet in them. And . . . my doggy's dead. She died before the plane took off from Rochester, and I was wondering if you would mind if I brought the doggy on the bus . . . I don't want to put you out of your way . . . and then we can bury the doggy in your yard . . . if you have one. 'Kay?

VIP . . .

I had just returned from Iowa, where I had celebrated my birthday. J.W. never lets me forget that I am one year older than he, and when August 20th rolls around, he's always there to remind me. There were a number of subjects on his mind this time, including a recent monumental catastrophe in Cameroon Africa, where a lot of people had succumbed to what was later determined to have been poison gas from a volcanic lake. Also, Jon couldn't wait to find out about my sojourn in Iowa. (The "Bonnie" he mentions is my stepmother.) He even gets into the subject of televangelism toward the end of the message . . .

BEEP I don't leave any name or number . . . I don't have to. When you're a *VIP* the voice quality is usually recognized by millions . . . not thousands or hundreds. The voice quality is recognized by millions of Americans . . . and . . . some foreign people. Uh, I'm just checkin' in . . .

The big thing here is, they're tryin' to raise funds now for the black people who was poisoned by the volcano. Now that's an Act of God, that's not tankers comin' off the railroad system . . . that's not people droppin' bombs of neutron. They claim that a neutron bomb was dropped by white people, but it was not . . . it was proved to be by a priest . . . a Catholic priest. He said that it was a miracle . . . 'course they killed him . . . they never listened to him. They didn't give him no chance, and he said it was a miracle because they would have died anyway. Now it don't make a lot of sense, you see. We all die, but apparently some of them, the tribal chief, Tattoo—Tattoo is his name, Tattoo Tooma—he said, in his native language, of course, that his people were pissed off. They told the priest that the neutron thing was caused by the whites. There was 1200, and now they think it's 2000 black people have succumbed to neutronism. But I was wondering how you did out there in the corn fields and whether you got any Golden Bantam, and whether Bonnie really kissed you on the mouth full? So call me now, and I'd like to hear from ya. I just bet you had a wonderful time, and I know it was an intellectual opening of your mind. That's good . . . that's healthy. You saw your old buddies you know. Probably the first thing you did was go out to the cemetery and visit their graves. Well, God bless ya and happy birthday to ya. I'll have something for ya, you know, as soon as you arrive . . . another birthday present . . . not pastry or cheeses, you know, from Wisconsin, or that bullshit . . . or an electric ham. You'll be getting a silver dollar. Carry that! It's a good-luck . . . the sonofabitches now, you know, cost about fifteen dollars apiece, so it's not a cheap-ass gift. Just . . . just let me hear from ya, okay? And remember, if you can find it in your heart to take any money that you got, send it to them people in Cameroon. That's it . . . Cameroon Africa. And tell 'em that a white man did *not* do that to them, please! Cry . . . you know, I'm practicing crying now because on TV Jimmy's teaching that . . . that a good Christian should cry. It's not a question of losing face. It's a question of showing your respect. So please, all I ask is sensitivity and a decent . . . you know, a *response* to my questions and answers, and if you don't, I'll take a hammer to your skull and bust it wide open as I would a steer in a packing house.

Andre and the Lamp . . .

Jonathan has always been a student of history, so his interest in antiques comes naturally. He has collected items of antiquity around the world. The character Andre is taken from one of Winters' "unique antique" experiences. Note the name that Andre has given to a type of lamp in the message: "Lamoje." Lamoje is real only in J.W.'s mind, but it has a very legitimate ring to it. A typical Winterism. At a certain point, Eileen returns home with a friend, and Jon has to explain his call or end it. Wisely, he hangs up!

BEEP This is Andre. I'm calling from the Big Oak Tree Antique Shop off Melrose. You were in the other day and had asked about the Lamoje lamp, and I told you that I'd repair it. I'm calling now, incidentally, from the shop. It's twelvish. We were going out for lunch . . . Ahh, Steven! Steven, just a minute . . . just a minute! If you don't watch him he goes, he runs in and out, he's cruising . . . We have done this thing for you, I think, at a reasonable cost. What you have here is a stunning piece of *Lamoje*. It's about the biggest . . . ha, ha, ha . . . *lamp* I've ever seen. I don't know where you expected to put this, but ahh, I'm hoping that you've got either a crazy outdoors or a gigantic palace . . . Palatsio Nova. Some of the little angelic figures, we just, ahh, I hope you don't mind . . . it's just our humor . . . we crossed all the eyes of angels. We painted . . . hand-painted . . . we put a lot of work into it but we think the cross-eyed angels are kind of funny and if you don't, we'll paint the eyes out entirely. 'Course, that makes the angels blind . . . more like Orphan Annie. Ha, ha, ha, ha, ha . . . [Eileen walks in] Ooops. Bye-bye for now . . .

Blind Luck . . .

Jonathan is the keenest observer of people that I have ever seen. He somehow gets inside them, and he can pretty much feel and think like them. It was getting to look a lot like Christmas when this message came in. Although it is funny, there is a genuine pathos that comes through as Jon assumes the role of Edmond Gerard, an engaging blind man. I wear saddle shoes and I jog—which explains some of the dialogue.

BEEP This is, uh, Edmond Gerard. I'm a man with a white stick, and, uh, with a red tip at the end of it . . . and a tin cup. I'm a blind man in the neighborhood. What you've done, Mr. Smith, is what I call really extremely unnecessary . . . putting not even wooden nickels, but buffalo chips, as it were, in my steel cup. Also pieces of marshmallow, some kitty litter, ah, you know, Friskies, pellets for parrots, anything but money. And you know, to screw a blind man is not good. This is the time of year when I would like to feel like the rest of the people down there at the Blue Anchor, the bar, the Playa Del Rey, all these wonderful places to eat. And I'm sure you've got warm quarters . . . but I'm a guy who has empty sockets. Although I can't see to read notes, I've learned to play a harmonica, some carols, some music. You know, people like yourself hope to skip by me unnoticed, but I know and I hear red rubber-sole shoes, those remakes of the old saddle shoes. You can't fool my ass, Mr. Smith. I've had people tell me, "Mr. Smith just passed you," and I say, "Oh, come on, I know scent." I know the scent of the male . . . blond, black, yellow, brown, Mexican . . . doesn't make any difference to me. I know the scent of the male. I know the scent of the fifty-nine-year-old, ya understand, running by, gasp, pant, pant, pant, gasp . . . I can't run because I can't see, I've got bronchial pneumonia, I have bronchitis, I have a . . . deviated septum. I have definite blindness. That goes without saying. I have a brain tumor on the right side, I'm going partially deaf, I've got Alzheimer's disease, and, uh . . . on top of that . . . arthritis in both hands and pelvic disorders, but my chances of getting through this Christmas are not good. If you could find it in your heart . . . drop me a *fin!*

The Tex Junior Story . . .

Jon identifies with the good ol' boys. One of his fantasies is to be a pickin' and grinnin' country star! J.W.

is always dreaming up plots for movies—this one comes via Tex Junior, who is calling from a motor pool camp in, of all places, Sylmar, California. Tex Junior seems to be, among other things, a fan of the California Angels baseball team, owned by Gene Autry . . .

BEEP Hello, Jim, this is Tex Junior. You probably remember my dad. He's been dead for several years now. And, I would like to do a movie about my dad, and I know you're a country western writer . . . of sorts, and ballads and things, but you could . . . well, you could portray my dad's son. I *am* his son, but you and I look alike, I was told. I was real proud of my dad . . . I hope you liked him . . . you remember him? I love ya, and this Sunday, I'll pray for you and the woman or the man that you're with. I'm livin' with a tight-bodied man. That's the name of my song that will be over the credits. I'll sing that one, and you'll sing the rest.

> *"I'm living with a tight-bodied man.*
> *A man that turns and twists towards*
> *   the sunrise and the sunset.*
> *The only man I know that understands.*
> *He drinks a can of Coors among the*
> *   rich and the poor.*
> *He wanders by the waterfall*
> *and calls his daughter Olympia,*
> *and they have a ball!"*

These are odd lyrics now because it's Sunday morning. If you should call me, I'd appreciate it. 'Member once again who I am . . . Tex Junior, the Rainbow Cowboy, in the Wagon Wheel Round-up Motor Pool Camp, and call me collect . . . I'll understand. See ya, old-timer. Now, a little salute to Gene with the Angels . . .

> *"I'm back in the saddle again,*
> *back where my home is my home . . .*
> *Where the cattle on the roam,*
> *and the chickens there near the barn . . .*
> *Nobody hurts a man with a pitchfork,*
> *you don't do him any harm.*
> *The Angels are in first,*
> *my girl's 'bout to burst . . .*
> *while I ride by the windows of my mind."*

None of these songs have been recorded because . . . they stink!

Sol the Agent . . .

I believe that Jonathan Winters is the greatest dialec-tition in the world. He hears a voice or a sound once, and he's got it. I have never seen him practice dialects or sounds . . . they just come to him naturally. (He laughs and says that they come to him supernatu-rally.) Now, everybody in show business has encoun-tered agents, and the lovable, traditional Sol is one all of us actors have encountered.

BEEP I'm with Sol Bernstein, my name's Sol by the way . . . ahh . . . Sol Bernewitz, but I'm Bernstein, Bernstein and Horowitz, ya know . . . like the guy on CBS, but there's no relation. But, uh, come on down here, why don't ya, and, uh, Mr. Smythe . . . ahh Smeth . . . ah Smooth, Smith . . . ah . . . come down and see us already and, ya know, we'll take a look at your music, and music abilities, and, you know . . . you sent me the brochure. Now is this really you? Huh? I mean, I get them all the time on my desk, a guy shows up and he's a lot older than the pictures. I don't want that. If this is you, hey, you're all right in my books. You got a good Waspy face, you know, a white bread–mayonnaise type of look. That's what we're looking for, you know. I'm not thinking of you as a solo, you know, in a nightclub or anything like that or Vegas, God forbid. I'm thinking of you in a back up group for some of the country western people that come play these joints in Hollywood from time to time . . . the Amphitheater, and the Hollywood Bowl. So if you want to do yourself a favor, come and see me . . . 2625 Hollywood Boulevard, Hollywood. And I'm up on the 16th floor, okay? And the thing is, you know, they call me 16th-floor Sol. If we don't think the material's any good or you don't cut it, then you got a chance to leap out . . . you know . . . a leaper. We got a lot of leapers. So hey, take a chance or take a jump, ha, ha, ha. In the words of my people, *"Chala Kahala, Lahala, Chahala."* Okay already, nice talkin' with you . . . oih!

To Patsy—
I'm leaning on this
chair because my "corrective"
shoes don't fit—
Love,
Jon
1981

My favorite eight-by-ten glossy of my favorite star. He signed it for my mother.

Grandpa Bellencourt . . .

*Grandpa Bellencourt is really Jonathan's grandfather
(on his father's side), who, according to Jon, was the
only adult male that ever spent any time with him. His
grandfather recognized Jon's talents, and gave him
encouragement and support. Jon loved him dearly.
Grandfather Winters seems to have been an aristo-
cratic, crusty old guy, but he had a good heart and a
good sense of humor.*

BEEP Hi . . . this is Grandpa Bellencourt. You
'member me? Grandpa Bellencourt. Well,
ahh, I'm you're grandpa, and I'm calling . . . let's see, I'm
looking at my old railroad watch . . . it's a little past one
o'clock in the morning. I turned ninety-eight here last
fall, ahh, maybe last summer . . . I don't remember when
it was. I'm not senile . . . I tell ya when it was . . . October
9th! And I . . . I . . . The cat jumped up on the bed here
a little while ago . . . I was watching the ballgame, and
I'd had my second can of Van Camp's beans, and as I was
watching the ballgame I let one go, and God, you
shoulda seen him! Nyowwwwww! Yowwwwww! That's
him, that's not me. That's him. I shouldn't be sayin' this
over the telephone, but I . . . I . . . wanted you to know
that I'm dying. And I thought maybe you'd get a kick
out of that, because you was always wondering, you
know. You're my only grandson, and I love you . . .
God . . . so much! You know, you only wrote me once . . .

I guess it was . . . last time was 1971 . . . don't make any difference, you're in my will one hundred percent, and I'm leaving ya a John Deere tractor. I got a stuffed great horned owl, I've got my ball mitt, and let's see . . . a picture of mother, *my mother,* on the *Titanic.* Oh yeah, and a bag of marbles in a chamois bag. A picture of me when I was in the war . . . I was in the Spanish-American War, and then I was in the war before that . . . I don't remember . . . I was in one war after another, ha, ha, ha, aahhhhh . . . Well, by all rights, I'm supposed to be dead by late Tuesday, so uhh, everything is in order. I got the will on me and nobody's to touch me. The coroner out here's a joke. I'm out in Walkerville . . . the coroner's the sheriff, the mayor, insurance man for North Western Mutual, gasoline manager, and the owner of the Brighton Funeral Home. Sooo, heh, heh . . . just contact him . . . his name is ahh, Carl Dohnler, and Carl will know if I'm dead or not . . . and come by anyway . . . God, I miss ya . . . hee, hee . . . Nyowwwwwwww! Yowwwwwww!

Danny and Darin . . .

After Jonathan had worked all day in Orange County, shooting some footage for the David Letterman show, we stopped at a nearby restaurant for dinner. We chose the place because a friend of ours, Darin Maurer, was working there. J.W. and I have known young Darin and his family since he was three years old, and I left a much larger tip than usual with Darin's buddy, Danny, who had taken care of our car. Jon caught the action, and remarked, "That kind of tip is pretty heavy for you, Snuffy . . . was that real money?" He left the following message later in the evening. Jon became a "teenager" in this message . . . cracking voice and all.

BEEP Hi, it's Danny down at Cattleman's. Ahh, Jim? Darin gave me your number. There's . . . ahh . . . the four dollars you gave me . . . humph, it's all stage money . . . were you kidding or what? I don't know how to accept it. Yeah . . . I turned to Darin after you guys left, and I said, "This isn't real money," and he said, "Are you kidding? Hey, Jim wouldn't stiff me or you or anybody." But It's stage money. It's okay, just the next time you come to the restaurant, we're gonna just slice your tires and cut your top around a little bit . . . and, you know, maybe crack a glass here or there. But thanks a lot, Jimmie, for stiffing a guy when, you know, every cent means so much to us. It's okay, I'm used to it, and I'll pray for you in church . . . ahh, this Sunday. Maybe . . . the following Sunday!

American Take Company . . .

Jon is mesmerized by some of the pitch guys that appear on cable television. "It's the old Midway Medicine Man routine," he says. "Barnum was right, there's one born every minute!" Here he comes up with a funny marketing concept relative for an audio-visual product. Hey . . . it might just work!

BEEP Hi, this is the American Take Company. T-A-K-E . . . with things around the other side of it, ya understand? The American Take Company. We have a series of twenty-four takes, that is, facial expressions . . . such as eyes rolling when people say to you certain things you don't believe. We have a picture of you rolling your eyes, either the right or the left, or straight up. Listen, I'm givin' examples which I shouldn't, cuz they're costly. But we have photographs, twenty-four black-and-whites, for what we call takes . . . T-A-K-E-S! I try to lay that on strong, because a lot of people are just dumb, and they don't know what we're tryin' to put across to 'em . . . Now, I haven't given you what takes cost. Now these are takes . . . such as frowns, you know, where the mouth is up or down, or the mouth is open, when you're surprised, or you're not really surprised. But this is not all I can give to ya. There's a series of, not only takes, facial expressions, but also a recording, ya see, of what to say . . . because a lot of dummies will not know what to say. They'll have the expression, but then not know what to say . . . ya see, ya see what I say? Ya see, see what I say, say? Well, okay, I'll show you. Now I'm gonna do a take over the telephone. ——That was it! You didn't know what I did, do ya? Heh, heh, heh, heh, you didn't know what take I give to ya! Well, for just $79.95, Mr. Smith, you get your twenty-four takes *plus* the recording, our recordings of what to say with the takes. That's right . . . $79.95. Send to 3001 Belvedere Place, Pomona, California. We know that you can use these, that's right, cuz I've only seen you, you know, just lately—you only had the *one* take, and that was the take of a *pissed-off man!*

Jonathan and some neighborhood kids.

Condition Orange . . .

Jonathan was a Marine aboard the aircraft carrier Bonhomme Richard, so his interest in and knowledge of nautical matters is no accident. Since Jon was an enlisted man, he likes to play the officer now and then. Jon and I, like everyone else, have discussed the dangers of a surprise atomic bomb attack. I had kidded him that the Marina Del Rey area, in which I live, would be totally protected by our steadfast Harbor Patrol in that unthinkable event . . .

BEEP Good morning . . . it is now 9:12. The day is July 1st. This is Captain Elgin Howard of the Marina Harbor Patrol. In two seconds the entire area will be completely orange. We are notifying you *not* to evacuate . . . there is no time for that. All people answering the phone at this time . . . in one second . . . Now it's already starting. As I'm talking, the brass around the ships, the masts, the people themselves coming up to see this orange glow in the harbor . . . it is not the sun rising. This is a total holocaust. Do not go to your window. If you should go to your window, you will be blinded immediately. We are speaking to you from almost 1200 feet below the harbor itself. *We are protected!* We have felt the initial jolt. Surely, by this time you've been thrown across the room . . . through the window near the pool area . . . on the grass, or into the harbor. We ask you to remain where you are. Regardless of faith,

color, or creed, open the book of your choice and at-
tempt to read it. If you have the kit #107-A, open the
kit . . . this will give you the dark glasses needed to look
at what is going on around you. 101-A, 101-A, that's alert!
If you are dead . . . if you are already dead . . . then forget this call. This is Captain Elgin . . . Elgi . . . Elg . . .
E-l-l-l-l . . .

Grandpa Sickenfoose . . .

*Grandpa Sickenfoose is a countrified version of Jon's
granddad. Jon often speculates that he would like to
buy a farm in the Midwest and return to the heartbeat
of the country. He has a healthy respect for cold
weather, however! He says that if he could find a
battery that would start a car at 20 below, he would
go back.*

BEEP Howdy to ya, Mr. Smith. This is Grandpa
Sickenfoose. I'm out on Route #3, and . . .
ahh . . . you promised you'd come out here and, you
know, thaw the horse out, and . . . ahh . . . the chickens
and the cows and everything . . . the cat, and even the
two dogs I've got. Even the missus . . . It's incredible . . .
we've had such a bitter winter. They're all froze harder
than a carp on a winter day, all the animals and crea-
tures and people—except me, of course. As you can tell,
I ain't froze. 'Course, I've been drinkin' gasoline day and

On the set of *Viva Max!* in San Antonio: Jim Smith, J. W., Keenan Wynn, and Harry Morgan.

night, and stayin' real close to the fire and the stove, but the rest of 'em . . . just like they was toys or somethin'. I just went up there the other day, the day before yesterday, and put a FOR SALE sign on all of 'em . . . who knows what you're gonna get for 'em? Call me when you get a chance, will ya, Mr. Smith? I'd appreciate it.

Folsom Blues . . .

I've seen Jon create an entire Western town in an impromptu sketch. If a movie company ever signs Jonathan Winters for a Western, they won't have to hire much of a cast. He can do all the characters—he'll become whatever the costume suggests.

BEEP My name is Edwin B. Scratch, my number's 782-590, and I'm in Folsom Prison. I'm allowed one call, and I seen your picture in a faded magazine, and it showed you, Mr. Smith, in a Western outfit and singing Western music and everythin' . . . Of course, this was, you know, back in the '50s, and so . . . uhh . . . I don't know how old you are today . . . Don't make any difference, 'cause I figured I'd like somebody to write to . . . and they've torn all the pictures of the women out of the magazines—the women cowboy stars, cowgirls— so, I've just been able to salvage the one of you. I work in a library, incidentally, here . . . and I deliver the magazines two, three times a day, to the guys on Cell Block 3, and so, I was just hopin' to talk to you personally and everything, and I've wasted a call, you know. Here I am, with just one call from Folsom, wouldn't you know it, you wouldn't be there to answer it . . . It's just another downer, and I'm used to it. I'm a lifer, and there's no way I'll ever get out. There's murderers gettin' out all the time and everythin', and shovin' people left and right, and rapin' ol' women, and molestin' children . . . and all I did was drive a car one day out of Tustin, right here in California. It was an ol' Chevy, and I sat there in the car while two guys, Harold Britewell and Tom Suckler . . . they're dead now, they was blown away, and that gave me a chance to go. I went about a mile and a half . . . I won't bore you with this story but . . . uhh . . . I stopped only because there was a Santa Fe comin' through this side of Ciderville, and I had to stop for the train or I'da been killed, and when I stopped, of course they come and got me. And I was got there at the crossin'. But it was an act of God, that was the way I looked at it, and I've become a Christian now. Aside from working in the library, I write sheet music . . . religious material and kind of . . . sleazy Western material. But I sure wish you'd write to me. Just write "Scratch," that's all, it'll get to me. It's Cell Block 3, Folsom Prison. I'm so sorry I didn't get to talk to you, cuz I just fell in love with your picture. 'Course, after being here . . . God . . . thirty-two years, I'm just as queer as a three-dollar bill, but I hope that I still have a heterosexual voice . . .

> "When the days that I still have . . .
> gone away . . .
> The chaps upon my legs have all turned
> gray.
> And my boots are brown from ridin' into
> town,

my cowboy hat is tall and dusty in its
   own way.
My eyes are set deep and my gun is at
   my side,
but I still ride Old Paint with thin pride."

Oh, I know it's all bullshit, but thirty-two years in prison, man!

Portfolio of Dreams . . .

Jonathan is a brain surgeon on this call. He most generously takes us into his busy practice, and describes some of his delicate neurological procedures. My birthday was coming up, and Dr. Winters suggests a number of medical treatments designed to slow down my aging process, and even throws a little "zinger" concerning the money he has spent on unanswered calls to friends.

BEEP Oh, hey, Mr. Smith, this is Dr. Winters, and I'm just in the middle of surgery here, but one of my nurses is putting the receiver up to my ear. We're operating on a man . . . we've been almost twelve hours now in surgery, so I'm exhausted. I thought I'd just give you a call . . . see what you were doing. You know, when you're doing the kind of neurosurgery that I'm doing constantly, frontal lobotomies, and also what we call "backdoor lab lobs" . . . or just using a True Value–type of electric drill alongside of the ear . . . This is probably boring to you, only that I know that you have always had a consuming interest in medicine of all kinds, and . . . aaahh . . . What's that? . . . We lost him . . . just lost him . . . It's okay. You know, you win some, you lose some . . . Nurse, just take him over there. Yeah. Get him off the table down there where it's cold. Well, I know you wanted to come in for some small facial stuff, but I don't do that. I don't do plastic surgery. What I can do, however, is draw out some of that gray matter that might be in your way. It won't leave you a slopehead, but it'll slow down your fantasies. It will also kill your sexual drive, almost completely . . . which I think is in the way now. When you're in the fourth quarter, and bearing down on sixty in a few months . . . ahh . . . the sexual drive *should* be stopped, I think . . . it just gets in the way, because you're asking for tricks, things like that. I don't wanna get into that right now, but get back to me if I can help you. I'd like to sit down and go over your portfolio . . . I have one here called Portfolio of Dreams. These are people I deal with, like yourself, who are uptight in traffic, and who are songwriters, and also comedy writers, and . . . of course, again, autumn people that deal in novelty books like yourself—or novels, I should say . . . novels. And ahh, actors that are tense and uptight. So, let me know, or get back to me, as it were. I can't get back to you again . . . these calls just about put me outta the park. All the money that I've made on the side is gone now from calling my friends, but call me when you return to base. Nurse? Put him on the table . . . Yeah, we'll get to him . . . no, that's okay . . . no I'm through calling Mr. Smith. Right down there! That's all! [to Mr. Smith]: Not for you to hear, Jim. I got a new one on the table. I gotta get some rest. Right now I'm going down to the kitchen and get some food . . . *that's the hospital kitchen . . . terrible food!*

Mr. Fox . . .

I live close to the Los Angeles airport, and I often jog on a road that runs along the west end of the runways. A fence separates the road from the airport property, and just before Christmas I mentioned to Jon that I had seen a fox behind that enclosure.

BEEP Mr. Smith? This is Mr. Fox. I could only afford the one call. My paw got caught, you know, in one of the slots . . . I got the area code dialed, and then there was a squirrel who was able to finish the number. So. I just wanted to take the opportunity to . . . ahh . . . to wish you a Merry Christmas. Now, I'll be out here, and I got a little red coat on this year, and a little black tie. You can tell me by my furry legs . . . and I really brushed my whiskers up, so I guess I look about as good as I ever will . . . And I'll be running out there . . . you know, they call me Running Fox. My nose is running, that's about the only thing, hee, hee . . . 'Course I don't take coke . . . it's just a natural runny nose. No, actually, you know, I'm Ready the Fox and of course a little joke is—I'm always ready. Well, you know when you live out here by the airport, as you know, with all the airplanes goin' by, you always get a little crazy . . .

cuz of all the sounds and everything. I don't know whether I should go forward or go back. I just run around here at the airport and . . . incidentally, if you want to send me something, you know . . . just send me . . . ahh . . . a bunny! I love to eat bunnies, and if you can find it in your heart, and you don't care what Doris Day thinks, send me a nice big white bunny for Christmas dinner . . . Heh, heh, heh . . . that was just the sound of me cleaning my teeth with my tongue. I ate some bubble gum. I couldn't get my mouth open till about two days ago. Well, Merry Christmas. I hope I can call you Jim, okay? From old Ready the Fox, okay?

In a Bad Mood . . .

Jon was frustrated in his attempts to reach me as usual. He had yet another idea for a movie, and he wanted me to help him promote the story. Jon was getting beside himself. He wanted to unload his enthusiasm on me, and I wasn't there to receive it. The phone must have been busy for a moment . . . apparently someone else was leaving a message . . .

BEEP Yeah, well, been tryin' to reach you. You must have been talking to somebody. Extensively, or at liberty, or whatever. And now the phone is dead again, and I'm getting this funky little message, in and out. I don't know what to do, Mr. Smith. I can't handle your career anymore. It's too much pressure for me, you understand? Listen, I'm tryin' to get you some mega-bucks. I'm tryin' to bring you into the future, and get through the Tunnel of Life. We're all caught up in the Tunnel of Life, right now, and it's a big wind tunnel . . . that's right. Now when you come out, you may come into the sunshine, or a bag of shit might hit ya. I don't know. I'm not a soothsayer, you know, I'm not that psy-chic. But . . . well, you should call me, and let me know what's happening. You know . . . I'm spending a *fortune* on you, on calls. Tells you of my warm, expensive friend-ship. Please call me when you get a chance. I'll be in . . . for the rest of the . . . *year*. Bye-bye!

Maudie Frickert Makes an Offer . . .

Jon says that he's a little tired of being Maudie Frick-ert, but I still find evidence that he enjoys the character from time to time. She's still saucy and flirtatious, and has a keen eye for the buck . . . like the guy that pulls her strings.

BEEP This is Grandma Frickert. I just finished a quilt, Mr. Smith, and . . . it is Jim, isn't it . . . Jim B. Smith? I've finished a quilt for ya, and . . . ahh . . . you know, it's got the flags of all nations, and I'm giving you the quilt for a real good deal, you know, $718. That's the materials and the time. And I've left a lot of little needles, you know, in my fingers. I ain't from India, man . . . Ahh, these things are hurtin' me . . . I was just wondering if you could get that money, or monies, off to me right away. I'd be obliged to ya. My nephew is still going through custodian school. He's thirty-six, and he's gettin' real close now to where he can fire a furnace and hold it! You know what I mean? Well, if you don't know what I mean, drop by and talk to him, yeah, Woodrow's his name. Well, at any rate, you take care of yourself, and I've got the quilt for ya. You get the money together, and I'll be looking forward to seein' ya. You know, you're a nice-looking man. I have always liked those incredible blue eyes . . . You know, you lay those on any woman of any age, and they know that you mean business. *God Love You . . . That's what it says on the quilt!*

Emerson Baxter, Driver . . .

I had told Jon that in my teen years, I used to answer ads in the Iowa newspapers, and drive other people's cars to California. I realized a substantial savings on trips west, to say the least. Winters doesn't forget anything, and I know that Emerson came from J.W.'s recollection of my story, as well as news of serious crimes that had recently been committed in the Los Angeles lower rent–hotel areas.

BEEP Hello, Jim, ya know who this is? Emerson Baxter! Yeah, an old guy from home! I knew a whole bunch of guys that you knew, and I still know . . . and I'm just out here two or three weeks on assignment. I don't want to go into what I do or anything, but I drive cars for rich people, and I was wonderin' if you, bein' out here in Hollywood, with all these rich people you know, and poor people too . . . a cross section and everything . . . I was wonderin' if . . . See, I rode a machine out here for Mr. Kliedel . . . I don't know whether you remember Art Kliedel? He was over there in Dow City, and right now he's a big shot in Sioux City, and he wanted me to drive his car out here, so I did. And, you wouldn't believe it, Jim . . . it is funny . . . I had blowouts! Them tires is thin! He's rich, but he's cheap, ya know. So I went ahead, ya know, and repaired them bastards, and then went on. Then the transmission blew up on me! He said, "Take it on out there to my sister, and then I'll give ya a thousand dollars. Then come back any way ya can." So what do I do? What I wanted to do is for you to put me onto some rich people out here. Maybe I can drive some rich person's car from out here back to Sioux City. Sure would appreciate hearin' from ya. I'm at the Finley Hotel. Yeah, the Finley Hotel. It's funny, Jim, it's like old times. It's two bucks a night. Yeah. You don't sleep in the room 'cause they'll kill ya, but ya sleep out in a lighted hall . . . in the hallway. C'mon down to the Finley and we'll git some broads and some beer. Be like old times. Ya know somethin', Jim . . . I still love ya!

Emerson Calls Back . . .

BEEP Jim, why haven't you called me? This is rude. Yeah, man, it's rainin' 'n' everything, and I'm in the hallway . . . there's a lot of leaks. Don't you listen to your messages at all, huh? This is extremely rude! I'm from out-of-state. I'm from your state . . . our state! Why haven't you called me? Good God, this is terrible. How rude! I want you to call me. Yeah, you better call me . . . *or I won't love you!*

Good ol' boys: Grandpa Jones, J. B. Smith, Jonathan Winters, and Roy Clark.

The Jack La Lanne Award . . .

Jon has always been curious about my continued interest in health and exercise. J.W. thinks I overdo the health rituals, and left a message making fun of the whole thing.

BEEP Hello, Jim, Jack La Lanne here, of the Jack La Lanne spas and workout parlors. We're picking names at random, and we picked yours as the typical middle-aged, almost bordering on *senior*-citizen, American . . . who runs, who breathes that fresh air, such as it is here in Los Angeles . . . who keeps himself in tip-top condition. What with giving up smoking and saying good-bye to alcohol, as it were, according to our studies . . . and we've certainly studied you on the beach, in your home, through venetian blinds, what have you. Working out with the barbell, the ol' irons and pumping iron, playing a little basketball from time to time, and, of course, with the little people in and about your community. An outstanding citizen . . . and our award from the Jack La Lanne spas and workout parlors goes to you for this month of June. To our favorite middle-aged senior citizen, Jim B. Smith. It'll be sent to you, C.O.D., of course. Bye-bye, for now, and *stay in shape!*

"I'm on a Charter Bus Goin' Nowhere" . . .

As I've said, Jon has always been intrigued with C&W singers. "I'd like to be a country star, so I could wear all them big rings," he says. "I seen one country star with a ring so big he could bring in one of them 747s with it." Jon has a perfect idea for a country song here . . . with a few lyric changes . . .

BEEP This is Malcolm Silworse. I've writ a song that I was hoping you might sing for me. I've took it to, you know, Steve . . . ahh . . . Lawrence, I've took it to Pat Boone, I took it to young Oral Roberts, Jr., and I've took it to a number of other people . . . Ernest Tubbs' stepson, or grandson rather . . . umm . . . Wayne Dillinger, now one of the hottest country western people in Nashville, and it's called "I'm on a Charter Bus Goin' Nowhere!" I'd just like to give ya a few lyrics of it, okay?

"I'm on a charter bus goin' noooo-
wherrrrre.
Pay no attention to the signs . . .
I'm on a charter bus goin' nowhere
down across the Mason-Dixon line.
They ain't no people on this bus . . .
yes, the driver, true,

but I'm on this charter bus goin' no-
where . . .
across the Red, White, and Blue.
There ain't no football game inside,
or baseball game at all . . .
I'm on a charter bus,
wish to hell I was on the Wabash Can-
nonball.
Ain't no people on the bus,
ain't no cheerin' to be heard . . .
I'm on a charter bus . . .
I'm just another turd.
I'm on my way to nowhere,
across the Mason-Dixon line
I'm on a charter bus . . ."

I've run out of time!

Tony Aphrodisia . . .

Jon loves doing a tough guy . . . especially one from
Brooklyn. I had been telling J.W. that I wanted to get
my '73 Cadillac painted. I also casually mentioned to
Jon that a friend of his was now a reborn Christian.
J.W. took these unrelated incidents and "connected"
them in this message.

BEEP Hey, this is Tony Aphrodisia. And I . . . ahh
. . . got a call from a true friend of mine, ya

understand? And he said that . . . uhh . . . you had a car that you want painted. Now . . . I want you to know I . . . ahh . . . I don't want . . . I don't deal in names, but I've done a lot of the stars' cars, you know? And everybody knows Tony Aphrodisia because I done a good job, and I want to tell ya something, Mr. Smith, we're talking about something a lot better than Earl Scheib. I mean, I take your car right down past the bare metal. I mean, I take it down to where you don't even *see* the car. That's a little car joke. Ha, ha, haaaaaaa, ha . . . At any rate, I was . . . I was . . . let's see, I went away up North. I was at Quentin. Ahh . . . for one to five, for spraying cars . . . But now I'm out, and I'm rehabilitated. I'm a reborn Christian . . . I was a Catholic before I was a Christian. I'm reborn, and all my paints have got "reborn" on em, ya know. Reborn red, reborn yellow, reborn green, reborn titanium white, reborn black, reborn orange, all the colors . . . purple . . . So, if you want your car did, call me. The first thing is, give me a little time to study the car and look at it. The last one I did was the assistant to the mayor. I did his. It's beautiful. $15.95 . . . 'course, I was crowded a little bit, you know. The man had some heat on me, and he said he wanted a cheap job. "Otherwise you're gonna go bye-bye!" So, I painted the car rainbow . . . *It's gauch-ee . . . Gauch-ee, man!*

Black Lightning . . .

On this particular out-going message, I asked the caller to leave the time. I had no idea that this single word, "time," would trigger such a response . . .

BEEP You know, ain't no sense leavin' the time, because time has run out, ya understand? This the Black Lighting . . . the Black Lightning person, and I terrorize people. I go all over areas of Los Angeles, Nevada, Arizona, New Mexico, Texas . . . parts of Idaho, Utah, Washington, Oregon and terrorize people. I do this for a fee! Now, if you have a person that you want terrorized, then for a package deal of $500 . . . that's everything . . . I will for a period of two hours . . . I will terrorize them over the phone constantly, annoying them, harassing them, or spend two hours at some particular time on their roof, in their house, waitin' for them . . . staked out . . . ahhh . . . I've got all kinds of things I ain't goin' into . . . I got a brochure with over thirty-seven pages of things I do to people for a fee . . . as I say of $500. This is the Black Lightning calling . . . ahh . . . this isn't Mr. I.T. or T.I. That's bullshit. This is a man who's been a victim of Special Forces. I've also been with the Green Berets, Black Berets, Blue, Red Berets . . . out there on the New York subway . . . I've been over 'Nam, I was in World War II, on the ground, off the ground, and . . . Give it some thought, ya understand? You may have a honky, you may have a woman, a transvestite, straight man, military, civi, or show-biz folk who's been an asshole to ya . . . ahh . . . you name it, man . . . somebody's been bad to ya . . . maybe one of your own people, ya understand . . . brother, sister, mother, dad, aunt, uncle . . . don't make no difference . . . if you want the person terrorized, I will do the job so that they will never bother you again. Remember, I'm calling . . . ahhh . . . from a telephone booth, ya understand, cuz I don't want any hotel, motel hookup. Somebody might record my voice or my messages . . . So, my card will be slipped under your door, and you'll be able to contact me, as it were, through my card . . . which is a black card and then the design on it is white lightning, and I'm Black Lightning . . . 'course I couldn't put black lightning on it . . . wouldn't even show on the card, ya understand? I'm a designer of art . . . and artifacts. It's beautiful to talk with ya over this dead-nowhere message system, but . . . ahh . . . that's how it is and remember, you know, you don't have to memorize after I terrorize, ha, ha, ha. There's no memory after I spook you, whether you be a Catholic, Protestant, or Jew . . . I will spook you. So lay $500 on me, man, and . . . ahh . . . your people, whoever they may be, will be in for a surprise. *It's like a thousand Fourth of Julys put together in two hours* . . . so easy, afterwhile, baby. I'll see ya later . . .

Grand Old Cathedral of Fun . . .

I guess Jon just wanted to extend some spiritual wishes from some prominent Christian media folk. He adds another salute from the American Sand Company after failing to reach me.

BEEP God bless you for being the Christian that you are, and on behalf of Pat Boone, and Jimmy Swaggart, and Mr. Falwell . . . all these people, and the people down here at the Grand Old Cathedral of Fun. They want to wish you and yours a happy 1987 . . . And the American Sand Company is sending you over fifteen million pounds of sand . . . *You know where you can put it! God bless you!*

Jonathan Winters with Sammy Davis, Jr., entertaining the troops.

Dinosaur . . .

I was using the "Dinosaur" cut from the "Jonathan Winters Answers Your Telephone" tape for my outgoing message. When Jon called, he was greeted by one of his own characters doing the Dinosaur routine. This is the out-going message that I was using: "We have an animal in the backyard that is at least eight stories high. The missus says it's a dinosaur, but she's been put away twelve times in the past two years . . . Bobby . . . go in there and git the camera [Jon does a roar of the dinosaur] and take a picture . . . Take it!" Jon responds with two different characters: first, Doctor Sickenfoose (one of his favorites), then the San Diego Zoo curator whom he calls Melvin Gohard. We had planned to play this cassette cut, among others, on an upcoming Letterman show. Jon uses a country accent throughout the piece.

BEEP This is Dr. Sickenfoose at the Longdale Sanitarium for the Unusual. This woman you speak of on the cassette has been took away two or three times in *our* place, and I find this a direct insult to mental health . . . [switches to Melvin Gohard, curator from the San Diego Zoo] . . . *This* is Melvin Gohard talkin' from San Diego, Mr. Smith. You're not to put these out on cassettes! Just makes a mockery of an animal that dates back millions of years before Christ . . . *before Christ!* We was led to believe that you was a reborn Christian and that you had a feeling for not only Jesus but for the animals preceding Him. Now, if you're goin' out to make a mockery of this . . . on this "Ledbetter" show . . . "David Ledbetter" . . . in New York, with that clown Winters, and talk about dinosaurs as if they was just idiot animals, then you're goin' be *visited* by these dinosaurs. So if you're just playin' with your guitar . . . or yourself . . . or in your medicine chest, or foolin' around with food . . . on some coffee, or leafin' through pictures, or playin' your recorder, or whatever . . . them things are goin' to stomp on your ass . . . okay? Better call me, boy, or I'll set these things on you!

"After You're Gone" . . .

This time I had backed my out-going message with a musical rendition of the old standard song "After You're Gone." The "fastest gun in the West" picked up his cue, and went with Morgan Sedgewick . . . a mortician.

BEEP Uhh, this is Morgan Sedgewick, head of the National Morticians of America, and we've just fell in love with your song . . . whether you ruined it or not, don't make no difference to us. It's a salute to the dead, "After You're Gone," and we feel if this is your rendition and if these are your lee-rics . . . and if this is your voice and all . . . we'd like to negotiate with you on the music, "After You're Gone" . . . because what we want to do this year in October . . . it's October 16th, to be exact . . . is the National Convention of Dead People and Morticians, and how they treat their dead . . . and everything. Also, they's a side benefit of a necrophiliac . . . them are people that "jump" the dead . . . and we would like to honor you, and give you some money. You can almost name your price. It's at Atlantic City on October 16th, and it's the American Morticians Association. So we would appreciate it if you'd let us know. My name is Morgan Sedgewick, Box 36, West Carleton, Ohio. If you'd write me there . . . okay . . . and the zip code is 91400. I sure would be obliged to hear from ya. "After You're Gone" . . . beautiful . . . just beautiful. [sings] "After you're gone and left me . . ." [end of song] See, I can't sing. But ya know . . . *I was dead for two years . . . Yeah, I just been reborn in the last eighteen months. I was brought back to life by a religious fanatic!*

Overcast . . .

A little J.W. philosophy and self-appraisal on a gloomy Monday. Very revealing!

BEEP The overcast now is taking over. I'm very down, depressed, and cold. The furnace is out. Ya see, we *all* suffer, my friend . . . it's not just the little people . . . the big guys get hurt too, my friend . . .

ya know? I've never known whether I was the little person or the big person. Physically big . . . but mentally . . . about the size of a pea. Give me a jingle if you get a chance. Over and out!

Shredder . . .

J.W. was looking to play, and he was not thrilled by reaching my answering machine (Colonel Ollie North was making news at the time.)

BEEP Could I ask a question? I think I can ask a question because there's no one there to receive it. So, I'll go ahead and ask it. Do you, at any time, Mr. Smith, review your calls? Does your machine own you, or do you own the machine? I think we're at a stage now where the machine owns you. It deciphers what it sees fit to decipher. It shreds . . . I think that's the big word now that Colonel North used . . . it *shreds* out what it wants to shred out. I have no way of knowing whether you're going in there to listen to the machine or you phone in. You have a lot of little mechanical devices that can alert you while you're away in the desert . . . in the hospital . . . in Arizona, Iowa. We don't know where you are now, and we'd like to find out through some party whether you're dead or alive. We would like to go through your things and produce some things that would be instrumental in getting me off the hook financially.

Pictures of us . . . letters . . . cassettes, whatever . . . I would appreciate your calling me as soon as you possibly can.

The Silver Stallion . . .

Our friend, Dr. Jack Silverthorne, provided much of the information for Jonathan's medical repertoire. The following message is Jonathan's response to my outgoing message saying I'd gone to a medical appointment.

BEEP This is . . . ahh . . . Dr. Edmund Lolar, and you've missed your appointment for the . . . checking of your anal canal, and your . . . ahh . . . prostatitis. And I was to give you the "Silver Stallion," you know, and . . . uhh . . . you didn't show. Now, either you were afraid or perhaps you overextended yourself and . . . uhh . . . were too eager and passed the place by mistake. It's simple to find. Ahh, I have done away with the Silver . . . ahh . . . Silver Stallion itself . . . the proctology tool. I have now had my hand . . . ahh . . . shaved down to the size of the normal asshole, and that way I can go right up in there almost into the throat area . . . ahh . . . the same as the Silver Stallion tool. Please get back to me as . . . ahh . . . I have about twenty-seven people in the waiting room, but I'd really like to get to you first . . . heh, heh, heh.

Turkeys . . .

Jon and Eileen had a slight marital disagreement shortly before Thanksgiving. Jon had a mind to spend the holiday by himself.

BEEP I guess you're on your way out already . . . incredible, it's 7:15. I finally got an invite. Yeah, it's a group of guys just above the Mission. I guess they're ex-Moose, and Elk, and Eagles. They said to come there. These are guys that have had mental problems, and I can identify with them. They said if you're estranged from your wife, or about ready to get a divorce, or just don't like her, or ready to beat up on her, and do something violent, "Why don't you come down here and take it all out on a turkey?" They've got, my understanding is, thirty-six to forty turkeys, and they're all twenty-five- to thirty-pounders . . . and they *beat 'em up, and then, of course . . . they eat 'em!*

All-Star Party . . .

Jon imagines throwing a celebrity party, and then conveys his general feelings about those in atten-

dance. (I have deleted last names from the transcription to protect the "guilty"!)

BEEP We've invited all those people over to our house, in show business, that you wouldn't have in your place. There's a lot of 'em here tonight. There must be at least 150 maybe . . . maybe 175. All *stars,* of course. They'd like to come over . . . and prove that they're *folks*. Their minds are twisted . . . they're sick . . . they love money, wealth, power . . . all that, but they're still *people,* ya know? Some of 'em are Christians . . . some of 'em. I'd say maybe 50 percent . . . Chuck is here, Pat, Morgan, I see Jo Ann, who has come by herself . . . don't know who invited *her* . . . but there's just some outstanding talents . . . Steve is here, of course, Red . . . some of the old-timers . . . uhh . . . sitting around and holding court. But it's a delightful kind of evening and some of these people, when you wouldn't have them over to your house, they sort of looked towards me and I said, well, "You're certainly welcome to come over to my house . . . the door swings both ways, you know." This's a Christian time of the year, and you gotta get yourself off to the good sound of the drum. These people wanted to know where you lived when I said "Not a good section . . . not a good section!" So long, kid!

Jon's star on Hollywood Boulevard—"another chance to get stepped on."

American Fox Company . . .

I had mentioned to Jon that I had seen a wild fox or two around Playa Del Rey.

BEEP This is Harold Maglin of the American Fox Company. I've set about thirty-seven fox loose in your area. These are semi-pet foxes, and you can pet them if you want to. The fur's worn off the heads. That's because kids have petted them before they was reared up. Kids by the hundreds come in there over the weekend and patted their heads so they have *bald heads*. You mustn't be alarmed by that. Their tails are full of fleas and lice, so if you take 'em to your apartment or house . . . the home of your choice . . . why, you're going to have to have it de-flea'd . . . de-loused. The body is molting because it's this time of year . . . spring. The fur is hanging loose. It's been jostled and everything. That again has been pulled by the kids over the weekend. Some of the foxes are missin' an eye. These are used fox, you see. There are thirty-seven . . . they're just odd fox, but you can get other eyes for 'em. They won't be real, but they're all right . . . just get ya glass eyes . . . human-being glass eyes. 'Course, they're larger than the fox's eyes so that he'll look bizarre. I'd just leave the socket shriveled, you know. It'll look like he's winkin', heh, heh, heh, heh. Better call me!

Go Straight, Man . . .

Jonathan was preparing to watch some football on the tube, and it was announced that one of the players had been suspended from the game because of drugs. Jon chooses the role of a black athlete to give his (heartfelt) antidrug message.

BEEP This is Woodrow McKnight, and I'd be playin' tonight against Ohio State University, but because of drugs, and bein' into heavy drugs . . . I cannot play. My brains have just, you know, been rolled out across the lawn. I want to say to you, and all your Caucasian friends . . . in the coming year: You understand, do *not* get into drugs, man . . . stay away from 'em! If you want to do drugs, go into some cave . . . or go down some mine . . . You know, sit out someplace in a jungle, or in a canyon, or somewhere you cannot bother other people. So you got no business with drugs . . . drugs will mess you up. My mind has been returned to me, thanks to God, and the fact that I've hung drugs up! So in the words of The Man, ya know, "A little child shall lead them." So let's see if you can be a little chil' and lead your friends away from the pharmaceutical shitbowls of life, you understan' . . . and go straight, man. Go straight! So happy New Year . . . I dig you! This is the longest message a black man has ever given to a white dude!

American Federation of Elves . . .

It was Christmastime . . . Santa, toys, and such things were dancing in the little-boy part of Jonathan's imagination. He uses a tiny, high-pitched voice for the elf spokesman.

BEEP Hello, this is the American Federation of Elves. Yes, we are calling our little friends at this particular time of year and wishing them a very merry, merry, merry, merry, merry Christmas. We understand that some of our little friends down there haven't had the opportunity to help jolly old . . . heh, heh, heh, heh . . . St. Nick, Kris Kringle, Santa Claus. We're up here at the North Pole, of course . . . well, about fifty-six of us . . . it's an odd figure, because we *are* odd, and we're using our little hammers and nails and putting together toys and dipping our little brushes in buckets of paint for the many, many children throughout the world. The rest of the little dwarfs here are just little assholes that are hydrocephalics, large heads, tiny bodies, small arms, bulblike eyes, protruding noses and lips, and large teeth. Merry, merry Christmas to you down there . . . and remember: *Don't eat the road apples, you're breath is bad enough! Heh, heh, heh, heh, heh, heh, heh, heh, heh, heh! Merry Christmas!*

Der Bingle . . .

Bing Crosby had been my childhood idol. Jon and I often take turns with our impressions of Der Bingle.

BEEP You know, it's your old idol from a long, long way from here. I'm up there above "My Blue Heaven" . . . that's right, it's Bing Crosby, Jimmie. Of course, we never had an opportunity to talk for very long because of my career . . . not so much *yours,* but of mine. You know, runnin' with Bobby, and spankin' the Spaulding, and puttin' one in the cat box really kept ol' Bing goin', and now I'm here playin' on the old harp . . . but one that's fairly large, and that you play with your little funny fingers. Well, I just thought that you might be around, and I'd kinda bend on your ear there, and find out what ol' Pops was doin', ya know? You know people can call you Pops now because we're talkin' about 63 . . . and when it's 73 it's definitely Pops . . . and when it's *83* . . . it's Pops, Pops, Pops, Pops! Well, whatever, I think it would behoove you, since I am your idol still, even though I've passed away, been gone for some time, and the old "Rug" has flown away.

You know, I'm just as good as I ever was, Jimmie. So, try to get back to me if you can. I'd like to find what's shakin' with you, ya know. You know it's got to get worse before it gets better. If it gets any worse, do yourself a favor . . . *and take your life!* You're only takin' up space. May the good Lord take a likin' to you!

Hot Puppies . . .

It was raining hard, and Thanksgiving Day was less than twenty-four hours away. Jon was concerned about the rains affecting the traditional dinners around the area, and he was suggesting "alternatives."

BEEP Heavy rains . . . heavy rains, my friend. The turkeys are all wet. I don't know what to tell ya . . . Many of the birds cannot be rounded up or found. Chickens are soaked, they're offering up small puppies in the Oriental sections of the city . . . Little Tokyo, Chinatown. These are puppies that the Humane Society doesn't want, so if you're short a turkey on Thanksgiving . . . how about a hot puppy . . . heh, heh, heh . . . or a small kitten turned over about twice?

The Black Whale . . .

Jon knows that the Black Whale restaurant in Marina Del Rey, California, is one of my favorite eateries. It gave rise to this funny Winters fantasy. Jon sometimes feels that certain people take an undue advantage of him, and here he airs these grievances by way of the Whale. (J.W. uses a black accent in the delivery of this message.)

BEEP Hey, man, this is the Black Whale . . . understan'? I don't want any more suckers on my back . . . less wise I'm gonna tear 'em up bad. I'm gonna head for the kelp beds, you understan' . . . I don't need any more mother grabbers suckin' on me. I don't need any more pilot fish, you understan'? Those suckers all over my body are slowin' me down. My ass goes out to sea . . . then I come back. You see, I'm gonna try to make out, you know, and have a relationship with another kind of whale, and when I got all these suckers suckin' on me, then ain't nobody else decent want to fool around with me, you understan'? This is the Black Whale . . . I ain't talkin' about no restaurant . . . this is the *Big Fish* . . . you understan'? That's right. You got no business givin' me any jaw. *You have to be some kind of shah to give me any jaw.* Once again, this is the *Black Whale* and *that ain't no tale!*

General Chang Wy Nu . . .

Jon and Eileen had just returned from a celebrity tennis tour that included China, Indonesia, Malaysia, and the Philippines. Jon becomes the fictional character General Chang Wy Nu to deliver an extortion demand. The General wants the money up front!

BEEP This is General Chang Wy Nu. We are holding friends of yours in show business. They are in the Wong Chi Province of China. They were visiting in Indonesia and Malaysia. They are no longer visiting anything. We want from you everything you have, in order to possibly get some kind of communication backwards and forwards to the States . . . otherwise they will be tortured beyond recognition . . . starting with the shaving of the eyebrows . . . the pulling of all the hairs in the nose . . . individually . . . then going for the teeth and pulling them out one at a time. We are looking for at least two hundred thousand dollars . . . *up front.* If you should fail us, then you too would suffer an unfortunate accident. We have heard of breaking the legs of enemies with the baseball bats. *We* use bamboo where we tie the subject, as it were, Jonathan and Eireen to these bamboo poles . . . then they are bent over like Indian bow . . . these bamboo, when they are very green, they bend. Then, when we cut the rope, they are then separated from one another. *I'm not just talking about Eireen and*

Jonathan, but the bodies themselves are separated . . .
dig? Get the money, Jimmie boy, or bye-bye . . . Bah bo!

My Legs Are on Fire . . .

J.W. is not interested in mechanical things, and there-
fore he is not very adept in their function and opera-
tion. Somehow he blew out the dryer half of the
washing machine as he courageously attempted to
wash his own clothes, and called for help, or sympa-
thy, or something . . .

BEEP This is Dr. Boernstedder . . . uhh . . . I tell
you, I have a tough problem here. In doing
my laundry . . . uhh . . . this is a doctor talking to an
actor, but I blew out the dryer. My legs . . . all the hairs
are burned off! I was hoping that you could recommend
some kind of salve. I am a doctor, as you know, and
you're an actor that would *like* to be a doctor. I know you
use salves, and I'm in need of . . . salve. My legs, I'd say,
are third-degree. This is just an expensive call. I'm calling, incidentally, from Santa Barbara. I just drove up . . .
I'm up here now . . . *no, I'm not up here now . . . no, I'm*
not . . . uhh . . . in Santa Barbara . . . I don't know where
I am! My legs are on fire . . . what else can I tell you? In
any event, you're not to worry. I'll be turning myself
in to some paramedic outfit. I think I'll start drinkin'
again . . . for what it's worth. Good luck to you and get
back to me when you can. That's all for now. Ten Four!

Monsieur le Général—Winters en route to the Carson show.

Universal Dial-a-Prayer . . .

Jon and I met a fellow by the name of Al during our meanderings. Now, Al was not the most endearing fellow in the world. As a matter of fact, Al became a burr under Jon's saddle. J.W.'s dilemma was in trying to put enough distance between himself and this pest without hurting the guy's feelings. In the following message, he comes up with a possible solution to his problem.

BEEP This is U.S.D.A.P., Universal Dial-a-Prayer, U.S. Dial-a-Prayer, and we ask you, Mr. Smith . . . we picked numbers at random . . . if you'll use and join hands with us, and the Festival of Lights, as it were, in the Christmas Yuletide circle . . . which is over four thousand people down in front of the Olmondson Gallery tomorrow night, Monday night, December 5th, for the U.S. Dial-a-Prayer . . . U.S.D.A.P. To get one person . . . if you can get *one* person out . . . that's a victory! It was said in *Von Ryan's Express,* by Trevor Howard, or by Frank Sinatra, "If you can get one man out . . . that's a victory!" And so we're dialing a prayer, Universal D.A.P. . . . dialing a prayer to get . . . Al . . . *out . . . of . . . town!* Please join us and . . . *bring your own candle!*

Free Flight . . .

Jon had been down with a bad cold. He called and made commentaries on a number of subjects. Jon was playing the "Baby" in the Robin Williams Mork and Mindy TV series at the time. I travel to Nashville, Tennessee, occasionally, which explains Jon's reference to the city. Buckle your seat belt . . . it's a long flight!

BEEP The time of the call now is 7:22 . . . the date is not important. It's always the time that is important. The mistake that you have made, Mr. Smith, is saying "you have as much time as you want." To me, personally, this means a period of anywhere from twenty minutes to twenty hours, which would be probably the longest call any Caucasian has received in his or her lifetime. My call is of no importance. I wish it were . . . other than to bring some joy or sorrow to a man in an apartment with a bicycle, weights, a few athletic supporters . . . plastic and some glass containers of over two thousand different types of vitamins . . . pills, anything from Bayer aspirin to sedation to pharmaceuticals that I perhaps am not familiar with . . . that have just come out on the market the last few days. I'm reporting to you about my current condition, which is anywhere from bright and sunny to . . . *grave*. The grave quality . . . giving you the bleak news first . . . is: the Commissary food is still . . . shitty! The bright news is that I'm still on my feet. I'm functioning delivering the lines. If you notice

Jonathan Winters left holding the bag for once.

probably tonight . . . ahh . . . one who is full of . . . given to me by my wife who obviously is . . . either trying to kill me, or is just fed up with my sneezing and heavy coldlike verbal expressions. Also . . . mucous membrane, coming from beneath the eyes, going into the nose area and down into the throat, is giving me a hoarse quality which will kill the Baby approach on the show. Screw it! I'm out after the bread and intend to pick up my check regardless of how I sound. But remember, like all actors . . . like ourselves who are sensitive, and not only sensitive to the quality of people . . . like Marlon, who don't talk at all . . . merely mumble with sixty-five multicolored marbles in his mouth, plus cotton . . . and who is able to mumble through some clouds which are not really clouds . . . but special effects . . . through an area where two or three individuals are on, probably, two or three dollies, and able to talk through a cloud, supposedly, to Kansas by playing Superman's daddy . . . That's all *we* pick up . . . but for that . . . the man picks up a little more than that . . . the tune of eight million dollars. Tells you that, Mr. Smith, forget your singing lessons, vocal lessons . . . I didn't have to go to Mr. Lee Stassberg to learn how to mumble for eight million . . . however, I've failed as a Magic Christian . . . ahh . . . through being articulate, I'm now out of the box-office goodies . . . But, incidentally, I'm told now by my wife who is very soon to be my ex-wife . . . That's not her fault, fut . . . uhh . . . faut . . . uhh . . . faut . . . uhh . . . sorry, minor stroke on the left side there . . . the head . . . the cerebellum area . . . going down into the ear section, causing deafness. Uhh, these medical terms which flash through the mind when it sees it . . . like a picture in the frontal area lobe . . . frontal lobes which will probably be removed before March . . . total lobotomy! But in the meantime, check with me on any important news you might have about the Ohio State–Michigan Rose Bowl odds. Should Michigan win, I would like for you to join me in the purchasing of a live Wolverine to throw it on Marcus Allen. Chances are that person will receive the Heisman Trophy, but in receiving it . . . his penalty will be . . . to try to release it . . . see how good he is . . . how fast . . . when the Wolverine is really thrown at him. See how many yards he picks up with that sonofabitch on his back. If the Buckeyes win, the Ohio State people, then that tells me we'll have to shower our section with Buckeyes and hurt the people. Buckeyes are good little, hard, poisonous nuts that can hurt people. Do you understand it . . . Ohio State beats Michigan . . . fine . . . there's a chance there that Ohio State will be going to the Rose Bowl. 'Course, Iowa has to be beaten by Michigan State. Of course, that's your people, and I'd have to be cheering for Iowa. What I've given you now is a little sports . . . some medical news . . . and some of what we call the mental–physical approach to what's happening on a daily basis. "Smoke Man" [our chainsmoking actor friend] is a total loss now, and his karma, as I see it now, about a D to an E minus. The teeth are gone . . . the eyebrows now are growing in different directions, which tells you when he does any takes . . . of course, ha, ha, ha, he has no camera time at all, but he wishes he did. When you see the eyebrows raised, or he's trying to make a point . . . the curling of the eyebrows . . . In other words, the eyebrows have to be cut. The man's hair is . . . looks like it's patched on by a handicapped person, and the lungs now, from what I can see . . . of course, I'm not a doctor. I made a point . . . I spoke to one of his physicians . . . who is a joke, and they're ebony . . . yeah . . . as a matter of fact, they're doing a study . . . uhh, *Ebony is . . . it's called "The White Man's Lungs Are Black." He's seated in a lotus position completely in the*

*nude, and painted on this chest with four hairs on it . . .
in his chest, of course, are just a pair of black lungs. Supposed to be the cover for Ebony.* I'll leave you with that.
I think it would be smart to circle on the map. Nashville,
Tennessee. Just circle that . . . circle it blue . . . and it's
like, color me blue, ya know? Crayon Song there . . .
something . . . I've got a little title for you. "Whatever
Happened to My Crayons?"

> *"What happened to those many colors
>   made of wax?*
> *The names I wrote on the walls*
> *of Peter, Paul, Jack, Tim, Jim, Jon and
>   Max?*
> *Whatever happened to my crayons made
>   of wax?*
> *The points are dull now . . .*
> *they don't write anymore, heh, heh, heh.*
> *Oh, there's one that says something
>   funny,*
> *something strange on my old playroom
>   door.*
> *Yeah, they're scattered 'round the play-
>   room.*
> *Some are on the windowsill*
> *and some are on the desk . . .*
> *Some are on the hobbyhorse,*
> *some are under my pillow.*
> *I've tossed so many out the window*
> *near that old wonderful willow.*
> *Whatever happened to my crayons?*
> *The many colors have all faded into one.*
> *Yeah, I'm afraid that one old crayon left*
> *is not sharp anymore.*
> *It's dull. It's the one on the door.*

It's the one with the arrow.
The mark is definitely black.
Oh, it's not time for me to go forward
   anymore.
It looks like I'm on my way back.
So long, old crayon . . .
I'll have to put you away,
to use you on some piece of faded paper
for my sweetheart on another day."

Well, of course, those lyrics have to be worked on,
but you get back to me there. This is a long message.
Well, give it a lot of thought, and in your lonely hours,
or moments there . . . when you're sucking on some vitamins or perhaps . . . ahh . . . some cactus juice . . .
Give me a buzz . . . call me collect . . . I can accept this
now because, although poverty will probably set in by
late July, God willing, I'll be able to survive the Christmas. Your gift will be a biggie this year . . . oh yeah, yeah.
It's not going to be, you know, a cheapo sweater . . . a
sport coat. I would say something in gold . . . yeah . . .
ya can count on that. Something you can say . . . "Boy,
he really finally gave me something good!" And it'll give
you a little some incentive to get back to me. [Jon re-
caps a story of two film stars who had recently been
found deceased.] In closing, I have a picture of "Jack"
lying face down . . . pool of blood . . . uhh . . . all
by himself . . . several bottles of scotch around the carpet of his apartment, and near him the life-sized cutout
of "Bill" . . . smiling . . . and the other is a Filipino
housekeeper with a real Hoover vacuum, and then we
see also in the scene . . . the picture . . . a commode just
full of multicolored pills and . . . I'll leave you with that.
Interesting that when "Mr. Bill" passed away . . . truly a
fine actor, all kidding aside . . . isn't it strange that . . .

here's a star . . . I would have to say and I'm sure you would . . . a superstar . . . not just a star . . . a superstar, and nobody came in to make his bed up. Do superstars make their beds? I didn't think they had to do that. You mean he was in there four days, and no sheets were changed, or pillows? Maybe he threw up on the pillow . . . uhh . . . were the bottles, glasses washed . . . or dishes? Did he eat out all the time . . . over there at the area he was living in? Strange. I'll expect your call soon. This is a long message. Good night, and in the words of Lowell Thomas . . . So long . . . until tomorrow!

J.W., LAPD . . .

Jon's road manager, Tim Bergstrom, is also an LAPD policeman. Tim has had a definite influence on Jon's interest in law enforcement. Here's a fantasy message in which Jon plays a cop he calls J.W.

BEEP This is J.W. I'm cruising around in the Los Angeles Basin on the surface streets, and I've seen a lot of action over here at a closed Fed Mart. They've burned it down . . . three blacks and a white dude . . . so we burned *them* down . . . heh, heh, heh . . . A little humor there, and . . . uh . . . so, there's just a clump of ashes. Car 36, black and white, pulled up in back of us . . . a back-up . . . and they said, "That's a pretty big pile of ashes." I said, "That's four guys," and they said, "Humph," and pulled away. But it's not good to rob even an *empty* building. Right now, we're in the midst of a holdup. I'm seated in the car . . . this corporal and myself . . . Corporal Gonzales, obviously not of my faith, but we're lookin' through bullet-proof windows . . . we had to put our own windows in . . . and they're just shootin' and shootin' and wonderin' why we're . . . heh, heh, heh . . . laughin' . . . heh, heh. Thought you might buzz me . . . I'm at home . . . right now I'm at home, as a matter of fact . . . even while I'm cruising. Ten Five!

The King Kong of Faith . . .

I had mentioned to Jon that I had attended a new church, which inspired him to deliver a subtle "be-ware" sermonette in an East Indian dialect.

BEEP This is Rauje Krishna Maugi Naugi . . . oth-erwise known as Rauje. Yes, we have heard of the Metro Church, which means nothing. We do not recognize this as Anglican, or Protestant, or Catholic church. Just a church. It is not enough. Why not join *us* in the Rauje's place? We don't even call it a church, be-cause many times you frighten away, for instance, Jews or Moslems that are used to the word "temple" or "mosque." This is just an old warehouse, but with a lovely interior! You come there to worship in your own way. We would like people like yourself, who are humble personalities, to come and give of their services. We need background music. I will be doing the voices. I will be leading the people. I will be what I am . . . the King Kong of Faith. You understand, I'm not trying to replace God by any manner of means, but I'm telling you that there's a lot of bread, as they say in the States. That's a big word here . . . "Get the bread." Please come over. We're at 2525 Neblar Place. This is in the heart of Hollywood, you know. It is up in the hills, where we are closer to Him. This is one of the most outstanding religious services of its kind. We're asking you to bring no money. Bring yourself, and your car. You leave your car with us . . . that's the only thing we ask. *I will give you wisdom . . . you give me your Cadillac! God bless you!*

Muscles . . .

Most of the local beach communities are caught up in running and working out, so the local gyms and health spas are quite competitive—and solicitous. I think that J.W. is poking some fun at those of us who are fitness enthusiasts.

BEEP This is Muscles. Dad asked me to call people in the business, people out of the business . . . people *in* business, ya know, whatever business. We picked your phone at random, Mr. Smith. We'd like you to know that we have an offer for you, a person that's interested in his body, and in his mind . . . like my dad, you know! My dad is almost 84 years old, and to look at him we're talking about a man only 74 . . . or 78 tops! His hair is *orange,* but his body's fantastic. Myself, I'm still working at it with my arms and legs and body. I'm running almost 25 miles a day . . . 'course, that's all I do . . . I run 15 miles in the sand and 10 miles on the highway, and then . . . of course . . . by that time I'm exhausted! I sleep at Dad's house the rest of the day. I'm trying to get it together with religious studies, but that's neither here or there. He's offering you in the area where you are, in the Marina there, his facilities: Jacuzzi . . . barbells . . . massages . . . and even hair transplants . . . hair retouching . . . or just touching, period! Our slogan is, "If we can touch you . . . you can certainly touch the stars!" Heh, heh, heh . . . And we have some *stars* to touch! So, we're talking about $58.75 for five days of HDT. That's Heavy-Duty Treatment. So . . . if you know where *your* head is, please call us, *because . . . we don't know where* ours *is!*

The Suspect . . .

Tim Bergstrom, the LAPD officer, has given Jon just enough police information to light up J.W.'s imagination. I had been out of town for an extended period, and this message was waiting for me when I returned.

BEEP Mr. Smith, this is Lieutenant Wiley Davidson, LAPD. We've got a MO out on you and a OM, and a ALO and IOT. We need some further information on your whereabouts. Our understanding is there's been a young man that's been holed up in your apartment there in the Marina. We've been keeping an eye on him for the last month that you've been gone. We wonder if he's a friend of yours, or you're a friend of his, or vice versa. We've got him classified as Charlie Bowler. Caucasian . . . height 5′11½″, weight 168 pounds approximately . . . light brown hair . . . scar on the right side . . . uhh . . . *two* on the left, uhm . . . lower buttocks area. He's been booked five to seven times for child molesting and also adult molesting. He's called Mr. Hershey in the Bay area, and also in Tacoma, in Springfield, Illinois, parts of New York City, and also upstate New York and Vermont. We want him, and we want *you*. Please call . . . Ten Four!

Jon on Muscle Beach reacting to having sand kicked in his face.

Dire Straits . . .

I had left a brief message on the Winters answering machine saying that I had been feeling a little under the weather. Jon left the following philosophical message an hour later.

BEEP Well, ya know, I've been trying to reach you now for . . . I don't know how many days! Eileen said that there was a long message that you were in dire straits . . . physically and mentally. What we would like to do is to run over to your place and see what things we can sort of pick over. When one is sickly and one is mentally and physically out of it, the great condors begin their descent. Just like great aircraft . . . they begin their descent to come down and pick off the bones of the deceased. Get the picture? And we want to know now *when* you're going . . . in fairness to us . . . when you'll be crossing over to the other side. We know that you're prepared to do that, and have been for a long time. I'd like to hear from you because time is growing very short for me now as well. I thought maybe we could meet and have a wonderful lunch at a top place. Maybe at the Salad Heaven or whatever it is. Saturday and Sunday I'm free . . . completely free. I'll be going over the *Moon Over Parador* script, trying to get it down. In any event, please call. You must do this with your friend. The other people are rented friends. I'm a true friend. I don't come out in *plastic* . . .

Salt Lake Calling . . .

Joseph Smith, founder of the Mormon religion, and I have the same last name. So do a million others, but that's all Jonathan needs for this bit of fun. He had, by the way, occasionally guested on the Andy Williams show, and met the Osmonds there.

BEEP Hello. This is Carl Osmond, the uncle to the Osmond kids . . . sister and boys . . . you know, the Osmond children. Of course, they're all growed up now. We've been trying to reach *you* for some time. We're going through our files . . . I'm in the second ward up here, in the Church of Latter-day Saints . . . and in going through the files starting, of course, with Joseph Smith, we came across *your* name, James Butler Smith, of Iowa. We're planning a big salute to Joseph Smith. We find that you've joined one of these crappy little churches that hardly exists, but that's neither here nor there. We'd like for you to come up here as the person you are: James Butler Smith, a direct descendant of Joseph Smith, because we'll be saluting *all* the Smiths. If you'd be kind enough to bring along a musical instrument, we'd be happy to put you up where we're putting the rest of the Smiths . . . about 25 miles away from the Temple here in downtown Salt Lake. There'll be three nights. If you could play your guitar one of those nights, and sing some of those songs that you've put together, the Church would endorse them. That might entice you to come. The Mormon Church loves to discover people. We'd like to discover you. Please contact me. My real name is Otto Maurice Osmond. That's right! It's Otto . . . O.M. . . . O.M.O. It's Oh. Oh. . . . And I'm not a direct descendant of anybody, except the Osmonds . . . *Mr. Osmond tore the guts out of clocks!* Please let us hear from you.

Musicians' Union . . .

My musical out-going message for the holidays un-leashed a musical fantasy from Jonathan. J.W. plays the part of Eddie Mandello, with a heavy Brooklyn accent.

BEEP Hello, Jim? Dis is Eddie Mandello, musicians' union. I was pickin' up on your singin', ya know. Happy New Year, and stuff. De ting is dat a bunch of duh guys would like to come over dere! Willie Moachler, Tommy Chinetti, remember, he does great bass? Beautiful guy. And Arnie Feldstein on piano. We'd like to back yez up to do, ya know, a little bit of *music* for your cassette on duh phone bit, ya know? We got a guyguy, for instance, a tenor sax . . . Arnie Bolshow. Arnie Bolshow is a beautiful dude man. I mean he's not *stoned* . . . he's not on grass . . . acid . . . or anyting. Duh guy's straight, ya know? Just blows a lot of air into a beautiful tenor sax . . . which would do nuthin' but enhance your overall musical approach, ya know? Please call me . . . what we call a courtesy call. I'll get back to ya, ya know. I hear dat from udder denominations, "I'll get back to ya" . . . but if you *don't* get back to *me* . . . heh, heh, heh, I'll be comin' at ya, man, with an indescribable series of events dat will circumnavigate your mind and rearrange your thinkin'. Please call me immediately . . . I'll have a song for youse. Ciao, baby!

The New Andrews Sisters—Bob Hope, Patty Andrews, Sammy Davis, Jr., and J. W.

Beat the Heat . . .

Jon's Toluca Lake home is located in LA's San Fernando Valley. The Valley heat can have you begging for mercy in the summertime. Jon calls with a weather report.

BEEP Like ya to know that we're *suffering* from the heat. It's at an all-time high. It's cooked everything . . . the enamel on the teeth . . . picture frames have cracked . . . incredible! Our fan broke down. So what we're doing is . . . we've got leather "wristlets" around our legs, and we *hang* out of the window! Eileen has lost her shower cap. I lost all the coins in my pocket. It's going up to 150 tomorrow, so they say that all wildlife will die! Good luck to *you* . . . hope the car doesn't boil over. Even more important . . . don't you boil over, heh, heh, heh. Give me a call . . .

Alan Goletti, PR . . .

A Jonathan Winters rainy day fantasy. Alan Goletti, his make-believe public relations person, thinks thatthis would be an ideal time to create one of those Hollywood "star" parties that Jon (and I) hate . . .

BEEP Why, this is Mr. Goletti? Alan Goletti? And I represent Mr. Winters and his Star Party. All gifts are *not* to be under a hundred dollars. Even a hundred is considered a cheapo present. We'd like to keep it, if possible, around five hundred dollars. The sit-down dinner is free, and many people are saying, "Well, I should hope so!" But there'll be favors . . . like gold pieces. Mr. Winters doesn't you know, *shaft* his acquain-tances. There'll be some people coming in off the *streets*. We're going to open the one gate to them, and they're allowed twenty feet before the chicken wire sets in, and the electrical fences . . . plus dogs and guards. Mr. Win-ters will come out at the *height* of the party and throw candy kisses to them, with miniature Track II *blades* in the kisses! Heh, heh, heh, heh! This is his humor! Heh, heh! We're looking forward to seeing you, Mr. Jim B. Smith, as one of his outstanding friends and acquain-tances . . . and, of course, your five-hundred-dollar gift. He'll be performing in his home . . . in the den, in the little room . . . so-called, the sitting room, the dining room, upstairs . . . in the toilet . . . *everywhere,* and therefore it will cost an additional hundred dollars to see the man pull of these improvisational *goodies.* Again, this is Mr. Goletti, and remember . . . let's not disappoint my friend . . . my client . . . the man I represent. What *I'm* giving him, believe it or not . . . a *ride* in the Good-year Blimp over the entire two-hour game at the Super Bowl! In the meantime, looking forward to seeing you on a rainy overcast day, and incidentally, feel free to have body makeup, facial makeup! Don't come as you are, heh, heh, heh, heh . . . come as you were! Heh, heh, heh, heh . . . *Bye-bye, Baby!*

Library of Dreams . . .

I had been spending considerable time at the library researching my screenplay, The Last Mission. *J.W. takes it from there. The character Shawn Uplinger possesses a sweet spirit . . . very sweet!*

BEEP Hello, Mr. Smith? This is Shawn Uplinger? Over at the library? Why, you've taken a *number* of books out, and have *not* returned them, books on the World War II aircraft and airplanes that bombed Japan, things of that nature. I have a list of the books here. There're over six that you have *not* returned! I have so many things on my mind, and now I'm six books, on World War II . . . We had a long discussion about your having them, you know. A "few extra days," as you put it . . . something about a goodwill gesture . . . And then I thought I'd *die* when you said, "How about helping out a veteran of World War II?" Well, I tried to help out the veterans of the Korean situation by . . . walking with them . . . to some bars. I really want to know what the situation is . . . so I can explain it to the "green" librarian, who is here full time. Are you going to *keep* the books and *rip off* the city of Long Beach, and we'll report you . . . or *what?* I mean, I don't know what to believe anymore. I found you a very attractive man, with a *sincere* look . . . and certainly a straight *pitch*. All I know now is that we're *stiffed* . . . as far as the *books!* Could you get back to me? Is that possible? Please call me at the Long Beach Library. Just ask for Mr. Uplinger . . . and I would be only too happy to reinstate you in our *library of dreams* . . . heh, heh, heh, heh. Please call me . . . It's imperative. I hope your first mission isn't your *last*. 'Course, if I don't see the books . . . it *will* be!

Midnight Cowboy Revisited . . .

Jon and I were about to fly to New York for a David Letterman show. Terrorist activities were being reported around the globe at the time, and Jon was facetiously suggesting that we take some other means of transportation back East. The truth is, he was less than eager to get back into the talk show routine and was trying to find any excuse to cancel.

BEEP You know, I want to give you some pertinent news. In order to protect my life . . . and yours, of course . . . we're goin' back by train. I'd like to leave around . . . the latest . . . the 20th. That would put us in there, you know . . . well, it's thirty-nine hours to Chicago and we'll train it in from there. We can't take chances in the air, my friend. This mad Qaddafi is exploding stuff everywhere. So get your train schedule out . . . or better yet . . . *bus!* I think what I may do is get a clubfoot, and if you can get your guitar . . . I'll sit against the window, and we'll call it *Midnight Cowboy Revisited*. I'll put the big glasses on and play the Dustin Hoffman role . . . but I'll be a better cripple. I don't think I'll play the glasses that thick, because I wanna really put a Protestant into this thing . . . I think the bus across the country will humble us a little bit. By the time we get there, we'll be *so humble . . . that there'll be no reason to do the show!*

Former enlisted man discusses strategy with naval officer.

Endangered Species . . .

Jon had been following the Colonel North Congressional hearings closely, and he couldn't help getting into the act . . .

BEEP This is Carl North . . . Ollie North's brother. I'm tryin' to seek some sanctuary. Not for my brother . . . but for myself. People are buggin' me, and everywhere I go they make fun, you know? They say, "You any relation to that North guy that's testifyin' in Washington?" 'Course, I'm very proud of Ollie, and I always say, "Yes, he's my brother." But I've been beat up so bad now in diners, movie theaters, parking lots, gas stations, bars, even ballparks, that ahh . . . I'm seekin' sanctuary. I was wonderin' if there was any place out there. I know that you're at Marina Del Rey, and that you're good people, Mr. Smith . . . and that you'd let me take refuge if I could. I'm like an *endangered species* . . . just like my brother, ya know, we're both endangered, man. Ya know, just like the ol' Marine sayin' which my brother used, "Just a few good men." Well, I'm looking for just *one* good man, ya know? How about callin' me if and when you do ever pick this damned thing up . . . okay?

The Rainy Day Song . . .

Another rainy day and Jon is inspired to song. Jon sometimes wishes that he were a talented professional singer. He does have an excellent musical ear.

BEEP *"I never dreamed you'd be out on a day like this . . .*
[sings à la Pat Boone] On a day like
today it'll wash your car away . . .
as raindrops fall from the sky.
Say good-bye to your house . . .
plastic car, tiny mouse . . .
It's another rainy day in LA!
So long, Mr. Airplane, as you zoom up
in the sky.
Say good-bye to Aunt Emma, Bobby
June, and Aunt Dye . . .
This is another . . . [big finish]
another . . . another . . . another . . . an-
other rainy day,
in EL AYYYYY!"

That's a print, boys. That's a wrap for now . . . about forty-five minutes. Oh, we can't break? The grips ate all the food? The Cokes? Well, that's all right, boys . . . it's a wrap anyway. Take forty-five minutes to get your brains in order, then we'll go right from the top . . . okay? All

right, second team, c'mon in . . . stand around and cook
your gourds out and stay under the lights until you don't
know what time of day it is, or your own name. In the
meantime, a little recording here. [Broadway show–type
of singing]

> *"Rainy days, rainy days,*
> *drive a guy and a girl inside!*
> *Rainy days, rainy days,*
> *in EL AYYYYY!"*

Well, ya see, there's a lot worse . . . not much . . . but
remember . . . *this is a former mental patient singing.*
Rainy days in LA. . . . Good title for a song! Bye-bye for
now, and get back to me. *Four thousand dollars in calls!*

"The Mornin's Chasin' Shadows" . . .

*A song I wrote, "The Mornin's Chasin' Shadows," is
one of my favorites, and I often use it to "background"
my out-going message. It blasted J.W. into a galactic
orbit on this call during a time when both Jon and
Eileen had been feeling under the weather.*

BEEP "The Mornin's Chasin' Shadows from My
Room"?! What if you don't have any win-
dows? I don't think you have any shadows, do you? Yeah

. . . think about that for the guys in solitary. I don't think they'd dig that recording . . . "You shall know them by their windows, and their blinds, and the antiquated things that run throughout their minds. Ye shall know them by their eyes . . . their ears . . . and their nose . . . Whether they're firemen, whether they're police, or just a "hank" of flesh they call a hose. Yes, ye shall know them by their fruits. Are they apples? Are they pears? Are they cherries? Are they lettuce? Are they carrots? Are they people with plows or shares? Ye shall know them by their fruits. Are they sitting in a stand, or in a marketplace, or in a greasy bag . . . or in a plastic place? Ye shall know them by their fruits, ye shall know them by their fruits . . . ye shall know them by their face!" Whew! That's a print, boys! Yeah . . . that's enough for now. I'm up here in Montecito at the country estate. The Little Precious Person came down with the bug, so I've been the male nurse all day . . . Today, on Labor Day, it's truly labor day for me! Looks like we won't be coming down tomorrow. That's the reason I wanted to alert you for the lunch number. I'm not 100% . . . I'm about 80. She's about 35 . . . Give me a buzz if you can. It's interesting about being the *faded star.* Once the meteor races across the heavens, and it's shot at by the people in the satellites and the guys with the telescopes, it's over . . . it's over! They wait for it . . . and then it goes, and that's about where I am . . . You wait for me, and then I'm gone! So these funny people have not called to inquire about her health or mine. It tells ya 'bout people . . . they just step over the grave . . . and go on to something else . . . preferably a limo . . . back to the depot or the home to see if there's any bread left. So give me a buzz, will ya? This is a hospital . . . Tent 4 . . . Unit 6 . . . 1500 cripples . . . and a *mental case* . . . Over and out!

The Blend . . .

Around Christmastime, I was back with a high-production out-going message, and had added my voice to a taped song singing "I'll Be Home for Christmas." Jon assumes the role of a record producer this time around and critiques my musical effort.

BEEP All right, boys! Right away from the top, I don't think this is the *blend* we're looking for. Ah, I understand what's going on, boys, but I think that the one singer, who is somewhere else . . . and the major singer, that we have in the studios . . . Smith . . . well, what we're trying for is a little *harmony* here, but it is not working the way we want it to work. This is not a recording . . . this is a personality clash, and I don't want that when we go to Target stores, and to K Mart, and to Thrifty, and so forth. So, I think we start with the single personality . . . that would be Mr. Smith. Right away, boys, from the top. Ya know, "I'll Be Home for Christmas" or whatever that bullshit is . . . but the other woman doesn't cut it . . . she's cutting one right now probably . . . and some saxophone guy is getting his thing steamed up. All right, that's all for now, boys!

Pink Grapefruit . . .

Jon and Eileen love pink grapefruit, and I had just sent them a box of this special fruit for Christmas. I received a thank-you message from J.W. . . . and then some!

BEEP Smith, we just got the *grapefruit,* and we really wanted to thank you. Had you not come through, it could have been disastrous . . . for us, not for you, because, obviously, you're coming into megabucks. You see, my book is doing well, but, of course, I've seen no green come this way. So . . . this has made our Christmas! We've painted them red and green and threw little pieces of Styrofoam on 'em and pretended that this was the Big Gift, you see . . . from many people. We're under the tree right now, and we're singing carols, and thanks to you, and the grapefruit, it's a happy holiday, ha, ha, ha. I hope you check in with us because we've got a big gift for you . . . uhh . . . even bigger than the grapefruit. Please contact us. We're up here in what we call Wet Montecito. It's very damp . . . This storm has taken its toll on the trees and fruit . . . the people. The ocean has torn away the wharfs, the ships. It's not a good time, but we're making the best of it. We're not complaining. We're just thankful to be here, you know . . . living and breathing, and looking at faded pictures of ourselves. So, please call us . . .

Pink Grapefruit #2 . . .

Another Winters thank-you and a subtle suggestion . . .

BEEP Mr. Smith . . . This is a holiday call. We've eaten the grapefruit . . . so we'd like another carton of them, if that's possible. We went through them rather fast. They're free, so we've been eating them all day long. We would like one more big box . . . same kind . . . this is all we have to eat . . . Please . . . if you can stretch it just a little further, we'd certainly love you for it. And, to hear your voice would be, you know, like hearing "Silver Bells." Please call me . . . okay?

Jonathan with Eileen.

The Beavers of Elmo Sickenfoose . . .

I had arranged for Jonathan to appear on the David Letterman show—specifically, to talk about the book of short stories he had just published. Jon always gets a little nervous before a trip, and he was trying to touch base with me. (I carry a beeper that allows me to check my calls remotely.) Jon's character, the anxious Elmo Sickenfoose, has a down-home delivery.

BEEP This is Sickenfoose. Are you gonna call me, boy, or am I goin' to tear your head off? Huh? You wanna go back to New York? Uh-huh. Well, you better return a call, boy, or we're not goin' *anywhere*, see? I mean, this is an *emergency* . . . *another* emergency. They're all emergencies, you know, when the telephone bill's on you . . . Here's an emergency for *you* . . . I've just set about thirty-six beavers at the base of all the telephone poles in your area for three or four miles in every direction . . . and they should have chewed them damned poles down by now! I had their tails dipped in starch . . . then I put a male with a female . . . and then, just about the time they were gonna *do* it, I turned 'em on the poles! Yeah! I want you to call me *immediately*. That little beeper on your ass . . . That little thing in your purse that you keep tappin' all the time . . . You better check in. I'm home. I will be home. You call me, boy, or

I'll tear your face off. It's Sickenfoose . . . Remember that: Elmo Sickenfoose!

Home Security . . .

LA crime had been on the increase, and Jonathan was prompted to install a security system in his Toluca Lake home. In the guise of Brad Wicks, of Wicks Security, he then entreated me (using a Jack Webb delivery) to have one installed at my place.

BEEP Hi, this is Brad Wicks with Wicks Security. I got your number from an agency. We're calling actors . . . uh . . . leading men, stand-ins, atmosphere people. Quasi-comics, comediennes, et cetera . . . young people and older people, people in show business in general. I got your number though Buck Young, one of our clients, and, as I said, I'm Brad Wicks from Wicks Security. What we do, Mr. Smith, is come in with security for all your windows, every entrance in your house. We give you a package deal of $385.37. That's the installation, that's the foot pads in the front area, and the back area, side, whatever. All around your home. All windows taped, and a code system will be put in, naturally, with the button system turning the alarm on or off. The alarm goes off, or on, when you leave the home, and also when you enter the home . . . Once you're in your house, or out of your house, be sure to turn the alarm off. Otherwise you'll be wasted, as we say, by the local police or people like ourselves. Thank you.

LA Express . . .

Jon and I are such pro football fans, we even watched the games of the short-lived United States Football League. Our home team was having difficulties, and the LA Express had been having difficulties, and J.W. felt that he had the solutions to their problems. He left this message in the voice of an ex-linebacker who had experienced too many head-on tackles.

BEEP Hello, Jim. I met you several years ago at the LA Rams with a compatriot of yours. I think it was Arnold . . . I can't recall his last name . . . I know that he was taking tickets to or from the customers . . . Anyway, I'm now with the LA Express, and we're looking for a . . . well, we're not looking for an *actor*, we're looking for a public relations man and . . . umm . . . we don't have a lot of money. I know you hear that all the time, but this is *tremendous exposure* . . . 'cause we believe the LA Express is really going to go places in the future. I'm talking about in five years . . . Right now, it's a matter of breaking the public in, you know. We thought that you might start out by doing . . . I mean, this is probably not up your alley . . . but I can give you a ballpark figure right now, so to speak, a term that we use, ya know, in the advertising world . . . We're talking about a standard five thousand dollars for a series of Sunday games at home . . . for six games. That's a thousand dollars a game, and what we're asking of you is to pass out some programs at the turnstiles. I know this sounds demeaning, but for a thousand dollars, it's not bad . . . I mean . . . they go through those turnstiles *quick!* The other thing is . . . at half time . . . to participate as a mascot. In this case you'd have the head of a pheasant, and a tee shirt on with LA EXPRESS . . . and then *feathered pants* . . . and yellow Adidas. Give it some thought, and get back to me . . .

Message from a Star . . .

Jonathan loves to perform, but he has always had trouble with the show-business facade that encircles the performing arena. I believe that this reflective message reveals a big piece of Jonathan Winters.

BEEP J.B. Smith? This is probably one of the most important people in your life. This is . . . ahh . . . I don't . . . ahh . . . I'm so important that heh, heh, heh, my friend, I don't have to give my name to some answering service. What kind of bullshit is that? You see, you're talking to a star. (Well, right now you're *not* talking to one, but you're having the privilege of listening to one . . .) And what are stars? *Stars are pricks!*

The real stars, the ones you see in the sky, we don't know about them. But we know this . . . they're millions and millions and millions of light-years away. It's the same thing in Hollywood . . . the stars are millions and millions of . . . of *years* away. Not light-years, just years. Not just across from the Valley into Beverly Hills . . . *they're great distances* . . . And, of course, what is the favorite line of a star? Ha, ha, ha, well, if you're not another star, of course, they just say, "Oh, should I know you? Are you important? What are you doing here? Ahh, what's your story? I haven't seen you lately." All the shit remarks. Well, ya see, I'm fortunate in that my star is just beginning to *fade.* I don't know . . . maybe it was bright at one time . . . I wasn't aware of that . . . because I was drunk. Then I was a victim of mental illness. I don't now remember whether it was fading, or whether it was bright, or I don't even know if I *am* a star. But I do know this . . . that I'm used to talking to myself and that's exactly what I'm doing now. I am now in Toluca Lake. It is now 4:18 . . . 4:20 just skipped. That's another thing . . . a star pushes the clock ahead sometimes to . . . make him feel doubly important, ya see. Ahh, whatever, Smith, I am at my residence here, and if you'd be so kind as to call me I'd appreciate it. Eileen is out now. God, she looks terrible . . . her face is filthy . . . her hands a mass of scars from weeding . . . but . . . ahh . . . the woman likes to do that kind of work . . . and, of course, I think that's what she's destined to do. Remember this, as the star closes out: He always has something important, hopefully, to say. Remember: Many times in life our grave or graves are dug for us, but many times . . . even more times . . . we don't have to dig the grave . . . we're dead and we don't know it. We're on top of the grass . . . not on top of the *situation* . . . on top of the grass. Yeah. And some guy comes along and steps on us and then we roll over and say, "Go ahead . . . everybody else did!" That could be your grave marker: "Step on me . . . everybody else did!" But why have a grave marker, if they ignite the body? I wouldn't even go for the urn. Just have people put it in a . . . in a . . . plastic bag . . . or just bake and shake is good . . . you know, they'd say, "That tastes like . . . oh . . . I guess not." And they go ahead and have the fish or chicken. But this is a long, long piece now. I doubt if you've been listening to it this long. But, I don't want to bore ya, you know. At any rate, call me . . .

Jonathan Winters—King of the Hill.

Hard Ball . . .

I had remarked to Jonathan that I thought baseball was getting ponderous and boring. Jon, a devoted baseball fan, disagreed, and told me that I reminded him of a very unathletic young fellow he once knew. The irony was that this boy's father was a professional baseball manager . . .

BEEP I feel that I can talk with you, Jim. I just *hate* my dad, and I hate the game of baseball. I've never seen you at Chavez Ravine at Anaheim, or at any of the stadiums around the country. So, I have to believe that you don't care for baseball either . . . I just *hate* sports in their entirety. Golf is a bore, with these people standing around in their funny sweaters and, you know, caps and . . . It's all bullshit. Football is far too obstreperous for the crowd . . . And some of the players! . . . It's just an excuse to kill, kill, kill . . . And then there's *boxing* . . . It goes without saying, with a bloody mouth, closing a man's eye . . . battering his nose beyond recognition, and eventually killing him if you can . . . They want to kill each other! The black man wants to kill the white man, and the white man wants to kill the black man. So, they many times just beat themselves *beyond recognition!* Tennis is . . . *Hollywood* time! It's a V-neck sweater, and yellow and orange balls, and it's just a *fashion* show! The other sports . . . umm . . . basketball is

only for tall black people. Some of them *are* attractive
. . . but it's not my bag to see a bunch of people run up
and down this shiny floor and do slam dunks while Jack
Nicholson strokes his head and adjusts his shades. What
I'm asking is to be a companion, and if we can meet . . .
oh . . . say at Nicodel's? Oh, that's in the middle of Hollywood, and if you don't know where it is, find it . . . find
it! I'll be there on a bar stool, and I can buy you dinner,
and we can just kind of talk about the business my dad
wants to be in . . . show business . . . Oh yeah. He's a
scumbag, I can't *stand* him, and Mother's no better. Myself, I'm just getting ready for the Rose Bowl Parade. I
do *all* the flowers. Oh well, that's neither here nor
there . . . Remember Nickies, and I'll be dressed in a Cin-
cinnati Reds uniform . . . Bye-bye for now . . .

Rose Bowl Victim . . .

*It was New Year's Day, and the University of Iowa
football team was playing in the Rose Bowl. Jon had
invited me to watch the spectacle with him in Toluca
Lake. I had to decline since I had friends from Iowa
visiting.*

BEEP Happy New Year! This is Howard Bonested-
der from Pemington, Iowa. We came out to
see the game and all. We just stayed over for a while. I

been asked to be a part of the Tournament of Roses here in Pasadena . . . me and the missus and the children. Reason you don't hear them is 'cause the flowers have took their lives. We're in my pickup . . . I put chicken wire over that and they thought it was part of the parade. They commenced here night before last . . . we was stuck out on the street, 'cause we's all drunk . . . the kids too. They just covered us with roses and parsithean and forsythia and chrysanthemums and pansies and everything. I can hardly get my breath now, and the kids have succumbed, and the missus . . . It was the pansies that pissed me off. They put 'em all over the windshield. If you just come down here and clean these pansies off the windshield . . . I'm goin' to drive my ass back to Iowa!

FDR . . .

It was in the early 1960s . . . Jonathan and I were in his hotel room, watching President John F. Kennedy conduct a press conference. When it ended, Jon stood up and reenacted the entire event. He played all the parts—the President, the aides, and the reporters. J.W.'s impression of President Kennedy was unbelievably accurate, and his total recall of the press conference details was mind-boggling. I asked him when he had learned to do the Kennedy impression. He laughed and answered, "Just now!" Jonathan's Franklin Delano Roosevelt is the best that I have ever heard, and I'll bet that it was another "Just now!" for J.W.

BEEP This is the late Franklin Delano Roosevelt, President of the United States . . . former President of the United States. This is talk from heaven . . . or it could be from hell. From hell to heaven and back again, is a story of many. Godspeed wherever you go, and know this: The only famous thing that I made up, personally, "You have nothing to fear but fear itself" . . . I want to say to you . . . stick it out . . . put it out as far as you can! And what will happen? . . . *It will be bitten off!*

Clothesline of Life . . .

The Fourth of July weekend was at hand, and Jon was inviting me to spend the special day with him and his family in Santa Barbara. He felt he needed some playmates, since at the time he was experiencing some personal family pressures. He used his favorite black dialect to deliver the invite.

BEEP You know what time it is? You have any idea? You don't know the time, 'cause your ass is still sacked in, you understan'? It's now twenty minutes to seven, oh yeah. Twenty minutes to seven on June 27. I'm high, 'cause I've gone through some *incredible pressures,* man! I know you're going through all kinds of bullshit yourself, with your own mind. See . . . you strung your own mind out like filthy clothes that are 'sposed to turn white on the clothesline of life! You done strung your mind out on the clothesline of life, ya understan'? Done strung your mind out on the clothesline of life! So I ain't goin' to get into a long thing, but . . . I wanted to report in to ya. I've had these incredible headaches . . . like steel bands around my brain, and took aspirin and ever'thing . . . Robaxin and all that, and my mind is *still* not relaxed. That's the reason why I'm callin' you. It's twenty minutes to seven on the 27th of June . . . understan'? I want to see you and have some fun. You can relax and suck up the incredible amount of *periphera* that surrounds this area. You know, the mountains and the chickenshit, and all that . . . the children. In any event, I loved your song, man [referring to my out-going message]. That's a lengthy song . . . 'course, *this* is a lengthy speech . . . but remember, "Your Brains Are Strung Out on the Clothesline of Life." *There's* your song, man. Sing that mother! Until next time . . . I remain yours truly, Woodrow Wilson Davenport Jones, the man who counts the white man's bones. Yeah . . . later, man, later!

J. W. and yours truly on *Hee Haw*—no corny jokes, please!

Epilogue . . .

People have asked me if Jonathan has lost a step or two. "After all," they say, "he isn't getting any younger and all of us slow down a little after we make that turn onto 'final approach.' " Yes, I believe that Jon *has* slowed down a step or two . . . physically . . . but I promise you, brothers and sisters, *mentally* J.W. has not slowed down one iota! I believe that Jon is a more exciting performer today than at any other time in his career. He is more focused, more together. (Incidentally, J.W. believes that everybody gets it all together just before we die. If that's the case, we don't want Winters to get it *all* together for a long time.)

Two years ago, I accompanied Jon to Pensacola, Florida, where he appeared in a Bob Hope television special. The show was to coincide with the seventy-fifth Anniversary of Naval Aviation celebration. J.W. was in high clover since there were so many opportunities to meet and entertain people.

Hope said that whenever he wanted to find Jon, he would first check out the hotel lobby. Hotel lobbies remain the perfect venues for Jonathan's impromptu concerts, and J.W. will work them any time the occasion presents itself. He can attract a lot of people in a short period of time. There is performing room, the acoustics are good, and there is an intimacy of sorts. There are no performance fees for him to worry about, and no cover charge for the audience to worry about. The management figures that the Winters appearances aren't too bad for business either. "It's the best time to work," says Jon, "when everybody is happy!"

Taping of the Hope special had begun on the deck of the U.S.S. *Lexington*. All the guest stars except J.W. were "backstage," waiting to go on. Jonathan had climbed into a roped-off area on the ship's bow, and he was doing bits for the sailors who had missed out on the seats at ringside.

Jon's sketch with Bob Hope was coming up next, and the stage manager was frantic. I got the fella's attention and advised him that I would fetch Jon, then I jogged on over to where J.W. was doing his thing. He did a half-turn toward me as he anticipated my message—"Yeah, I know, Mr. Smith. I'm on my way"—and assured his enamored audience that he would return.

There was tremendous applause when Jon took the stage with Hope. And after the two comedians performed their scene, the audience roared its approval. As soon as he finished the on-camera scene, Jon returned to his buddies on the bow of the ship. The Hope special was just sort of an *aside* to J.W. . . . an interruption really. A paying one, however, and that's the reason Jon honored it.

The Florida festivities came to an end, too soon for J.W. and me. We were having a good time. A Pensacola newspaper printed the bottom line on Jon's visit: "During his stay in Pensacola, Winters won the hearts of people who heard his impromptu stories at the Pensacola Hilton, local restaurants, and the Pensacola Civic Center."

Jonathan and I boarded the great silver bird for our trip back to LA . . . Our airplane had just reached cruising altitude when Jon began rummaging around in his carry-on bag. He pulled out a World War II pilot's cap, complete with goggles. I knew, without asking, that Jon was headed for the coach section to perform for the folks. "Aren't you a little bushed, Mr. Winters?" I queried. Jon smiled. "You gotta make people happy, Mr. Smith!"

I didn't see J.W. again until we had arrived at the gate. I caught up with him in coach. Jon was grinning with satisfaction as he stuffed his headgear back into its bag. He waved at the laughing passengers and started for the gate ramp. Someone turned to me and said, "He gives pleasure to a lot of people." "He's the best," I agreed. "He's King of the Hill!" The fellow smiled and gave me a thumbs-up as he repeated the words: "King of the Hill!"